THE CASE
FOR
JUSTICE

Gerald M. Pops
Thomas J. Pavlak

THE CASE
FOR
JUSTICE

*Strengthening Decision
Making and Policy in
Public Administration*

Jossey-Bass Publishers

San Francisco • Oxford • 1991

THE CASE FOR JUSTICE
Strengthening Decision Making and Policy in Public Administration
by Gerald M. Pops and Thomas J. Pavlak

Copyright © 1991 by: Jossey-Bass Inc., Publishers
350 Sansome Street
San Francisco, California 94104
&
Jossey-Bass Limited
Headington Hill Hall
Oxford OX3 0BW

Library of Congress Cataloging-in-Publication Data

Pops, Gerald M.
    The case for justice : strengthening decision making and policy in
public administration / Gerald M. Pops and Thomas J. Pavlak.
        p.   cm. — (The Jossey-Bass public administration series)
    Includes bibliographic references and index.
    ISBN 1-55542-375-2
    1. Public administration—Decision making. 2. Administrative law.
3. Justice. I. Pavlak, Thomas J. II. Title. III. Series.
JF1525.D4P67   1991
350.007'25—dc20   91-12793
                                                                        CIP

Manufactured in the United States of America

JACKET DESIGN BY WILLI BAUM

FIRST EDITION

Code 9174

The Jossey-Bass
Public Administration Series

Tzedek, tzedek, tir'defu
"Justice, only justice shall you pursue."

Deuteronomy 16:20

CONTENTS

To Marcia and Christine

For whose constant encouragement and sacrifice
we are grateful.

PREFACE

This is a book about justice. More particularly, this is a book about the demands justice makes on public organizations and on public administrators as individuals. Since the late 1930s, it has been assumed that justice does not really have very much to do with being a public servant or a public manager. Rather, justice is said to be the business of the courts and the legal profession. Agencies are expected to hire lawyers who operate the formalized hearings that are part and parcel of administrative decision processes. Lawyers represent agencies in the courts and reduce the chances that they will be sued.

Justice is also thought to be very much the business of elected officials, those legislators and chief executives who act to create the law within the constraints imposed by constitutions, elections, and public opinion. The public policies fashioned by these democratically elected officials distribute benefits and burdens in society. This is called social justice. If the injustice of a particular law in its design or application is felt, it might rationally be attributed to the executive and legislative branches. But in truth, part of the blame is heaped upon the administrative agencies that attempt to carry the law into effect.

How much influence can public administrators have in mitigating the injustices of a world that, by the time they get to it, is already unfair in many ways? When citizens and interest groups suffer negative consequences as the result of government programs, they will normally direct their complaints first at the agencies that administer the programs. Far too often legislators and elected executives are quick to agree and to reinforce that perception, lest they themselves be the primary targets of discontent. Despite the finger pointing, the bureaucracy is far less culpable than it is made out to be. Often, it is the natural consequences of the lawmakers' plan that generate the complaints. Thus we have a situation in which public administrators shoulder much of the blame when there is a breakdown in social justice but have limited participation in the essentially lawyer-dominated systems that exist for rectifying injustice when it is found at the administrative level.

Of course, public administration is not neutral in the matter of governmental justice and injustice but is itself a major policymaker, although it is clear that the founders did not intend it to be. Its power to do justice and injustice has grown apace with the enormous growth in the power of the administrative state in the twentieth century. Escalating rights of citizens and expectations of fair treatment at the hands of government have come to be a large part of the environment within which public agencies operate.

Beyond their limited ability to "make" policy, public agencies and public administrators are important, and their crucial role in implementation can shape public policy. They are the contact between government and the people, and the way they apply the law and operate the programs they are given will often determine whether the citizenry sees government as responsive and fair. They have the opportunity to make policies more flexible, to make legitimate exceptions, and to be responsive to citizen needs.

As a group of actors, public administrators probably have a less optimistic view of their ability to make a difference in delivering a more just society than they have had in the past. During the New Deal of the 1930s when government was seen as a positive force in helping the nation overcome the Great Depression, in the 1960s when President Kennedy called the nation's "best and brightest" to government service, and again in the optimistic era of the expanded welfare programs of the Great Society, public administration was more self-confident and the American people prouder of their public service. But such days seem shrouded in the past, and public servants are themselves part of a society that has come to question the right of the public service to be expansive and proactive.

It is possible that this view may be changing. With the winding down of the "Reagan revolution" that sought private solutions to social problems and preached that government is part of the problem, more positive views about the proper ends of government would seem appropriate. This view is consistent with the increased concern for ethical behavior in both public policy and public administration. At this juncture, a book that asserts that government should redirect its efforts toward promoting justice is fitting.

Our first task, then, is to convince the reader that justice is a worthy, reasonable, and practical value for public administration to pursue. The second task is to show the role public administration has had in shaping justice in the past. As part of that demonstration, it will be necessary to explore the subject of administrative law and to make that subject more understandable and its content more accessible to the larger public administration community. As a subject matter, public administration education has usually relegated administrative law to a peripheral position, with two unfortunate results. First, its importance in explaining how administrative decisions are made has not been sufficiently appreciated. Second, the assumption that administrative law ought to dominate the matter of justice in public organizations has not been questioned.

There has been one other motivation for writing this book. It is our belief that justice ought to be a determinative factor in the making of administrative decisions, a factor that public administration education and practice have overlooked. Justice issues now play an enormous role in the operation of our public organizations, despite the fact that the role of public administration in affecting and effecting justice is neither well understood nor effectively acted upon. If we are able to define a common theoretical basis and approach to these issues, we will have advanced the study of administrative decision making in general. We hope that our diverse educational and practitioner backgrounds, as well as our broad knowledge of and perspectives on public administration, have helped to develop a text to this end.

Overview of the Contents

In presenting a justice approach to public organization decision making, we have chosen to be accessible to a wide audience. This requires painting with broad brush strokes a picture that in actuality is quite complex and rich in texture and detail. Our purpose has been more to stimulate thinking about administrative justice issues than to catalogue and analyze the many and often quite fascinating justice-laden issues that arise in administrative settings. It is tempting to venture into doorways labeled affirmative action, comparable worth, whistle-blowing, and grievance procedures, but we leave this exploration for other observers more expert and practiced in the intricacies of such topics. Seeking to map the terrain broadly, we have instead concentrated on the central phenomenon of the role that justice plays and ought to play in the decision making of public organizations.

A second feature is that we are here concerned primarily with a broad range of disputes that administrative agencies have both with citizens and with their own employees. It is in this zone that the need for justice is greatest and the concept of justice the most visible and understandable, given our nation's historical regard for individual rights. We give less attention to other aspects of administration, such as the decisions involved in the planning, budgeting, and personnel processes of public agencies, but these too are concerned with justice.

Although we are mindful of the formal adjudication process—the detailed workings of hearings, grievance proce-

dures, and arbitration—it is the basic principles of justice
that catch and hold our attention. We wish to focus on what
public managers and agency leaders can do in the great
majority of cases that never reach or need to reach the formal
process to promote the ends of justice. We have, as a result,
deliberately given less space to the procedural trappings of
formalized decision making, such as the scope or conduct of
hearings, the duties and organization of state and federal
administrative law judge corps, the working of administrative
law, or the techniques and strategies employed by administrative lawyers.

Finally, we seek to offer public managers an overview
on their actions when confronted with a justice issue, rather
than a set of specific prescriptive guidelines. The problem
facing public administrators is not that there is a lack of
guidelines for administrative action. If anything, administrators have too many guidelines to follow; statutes, agency rules
and regulations, court rulings, and ethics codes all contain
prescriptions for administrative behavior. What is needed
is a "metaguide" for administrative decision making, one
that can assist administrators in sorting through the myriad
guides that may be operative in any decision context. We present our administrative justice principles in this spirit.

Chapter One will introduce the major themes of the
book, which include claims about the critical importance of
the concept of justice in public administration, the scope and
nature of administrative justice, and the utility of that concept as an organizing approach to a variety of decisions in
public organizations.

Chapter Two discusses the crucial role that administrative law has played in defining and determining our notions
about the subject of administrative justice. Chapter Three
looks at alternative visions of administrative justice, beginning with the views of legal reform scholars who challenge
prevailing institutions and practices of administrative law
and proceeding to the work of social psychologists, labor relations and conflict resolution writers, and public administration scholars. It summarizes a good deal of conceptualization

that has allowed us to move toward a redefinition of administrative justice.

Chapters Four, Five, and Six contain our perspective of a model of administrative justice. In Chapter Four, we illustrate the criteria for a just decision and their application. The building of a just organization, focusing on obstacles and opportunities, is considered in Chapter Five. We discuss the molding of a just public administrator in Chapter Six, in which the consequences of the model are spelled out in a variety of public administrator roles.

Chapter Seven considers the causes and types of injustice with which public organizations have to contend. In a sense, such considerations precede the formulation of the administrative justice model by helping to lay a foundation for its need. In another sense, a consideration of the remedy to the sense of injustice inherent in our society takes us beyond the problem of designing an administrative justice model to the kinds of attitudes to be cultivated if a government agency is to be perceived as just. Chapter Eight, the concluding chapter, pulls all of the foregoing matters together and reinforces our argument that a normative theory and practice of administrative justice is possible and necessary.

Acknowledgments

This book would not be complete without acknowledging those who have helped us. Henry Kass and David Williams, cochairs of the Department of Public Administration at West Virginia University, were early and enthusiastic supporters. Both David Williams and Leon Haley, former acting dean of the Graduate School of Public and International Affairs, provided time off from teaching and travel funds.

Max O. Stephenson, Jr., William N. Dunn, and Richard Sylves read and gave helpful comments on early draft chapters. Two anonymous Jossey-Bass reviewers read the entire manuscript and made recommendations that markedly improved the final book.

Scott Marshall helped develop case examples, and he, Cheron Watchman, and Richard Basom assisted with library research. Deborah Koon and Pamela Turner edited and reproduced the final draft and they, along with Willie Gianfrancesco, performed a variety of clerical duties throughout the project.

June 1991   Gerald M. Pops
                                               Morgantown, West Virginia

                                               Thomas J. Pavlak
                                               New York, New York

THE AUTHORS

Gerald M. Pops is professor of public administration at West Virginia University. He received his B.A.
degree (1957) from the University of California, Los Angeles,
in political science; his law degree (1961) from the University
of California, Berkeley; and his Ph.D. degree (1974) from the
Maxwell School at Syracuse University in public administration. Prior to commencing his academic career, he served as a
judge advocate and trial attorney for the U.S. Air Force and
as an administrative analyst in the Office of the Legislative
Analyst for the California legislature.

Pops's interest in administrative justice dates from the
1960s, when he became involved as counsel in administrative
proceedings relating to discharge from the U.S. Air Force and
with the process used in the California legislature for processing citizen equity claims against the state. His recent
scholarship has focused on administrative law and process,
the role of conflict in public management, and administrative
ethics. He is the author of *Emergence of the Public Sector
Arbitrator* (1976) and coauthor of *Conflict Resolution in the
Policy Process* (1987, with Max O. Stephenson, Jr.).

Thomas J. Pavlak is professor of public administration and director of the Public Administration Institute at Fairleigh Dickinson University. He received his B.A.

degree (1965) in social studies, as well as his M.A. and Ph.D. degrees (1968, 1971) in political science, from the University of Illinois, Urbana-Champaign.

Prior to joining the faculty of Fairleigh Dickinson University in 1989, Pavlak served as director of both doctoral studies and the Public Management and Policy Program at the University of Pittsburgh's Graduate School of Public and International Affairs. In addition, he has been a National Association of Schools of Public Affairs and Administration Fellow at the U.S. Department of Housing and Urban Development, a visiting faculty fellow at the National Institute of Justice, and a Navy/American Society for Engineering Education Faculty Fellow at the U.S. Navy Personnel Research and Development Center.

Pavlak's interest in administrative justice began in the mid 1970s, when he collaborated on projects with Jerry L. Mashaw, Paul Verkuil, and other prominent administrative law scholars at the National Center for Administrative Justice. His research on administrative justice issues includes studies of school disciplinary suspensions, parole revocation, and prison discipline. His recent publications include articles on workplace grievance procedures and AIDS in the workplace.

THE CASE
FOR
JUSTICE

1

WHY
JUSTICE MATTERS
IN PUBLIC
ADMINISTRATION

When Gladys Burr died recently, the *New York Times* noted her passing. In many respects, hers was an unremarkable life, hardly the stuff of interest for a national newspaper. And yet, Gladys Burr's life was unique in a tragic, shocking way. What made her passing a newsworthy event is a single, compelling fact about her life: Gladys Burr spent forty-two years in Connecticut state mental institutions after being mistakenly classified mentally retarded. To compound this Kafkaesque horror, officials knew for more than thirty years that she was not retarded.

The FBI and the Environmental Protection Agency (EPA) are investigating possible felony violations of federal laws at the Rocky Flats, Colorado, atomic weapons plant. In operation since 1951, the plant is owned by the Department of Energy (DOE) and managed by a contractor, Rockwell International Corporation. The FBI says it has probable cause to believe that DOE and Rockwell officials falsely certified that some plant facilities were in compliance with the law, that they made false statements and concealed material

1

facts, and that hazardous chemical and radioactive waste were illegally treated, stored, and disposed of at Rocky Flats.

A recent Social Security Administration (SSA) study revealed that tens of thousands of poor persons who are aged, who are blind, or who have disabilities were wrongly dropped from the Supplemental Security Income (SSI) program. According to the SSA study, 84 percent of those dropped from the program's rolls should not have been terminated. In a high percentage of cases, SSA field officers did not follow the agency's procedures for suspending benefits. For many of these recipients, SSI payments were their sole income, and removal from the program resulted in extreme hardship. The agency concluded that the problem was related to staff cuts and an increasing workload.

These are difficult times for public managers. Government at all levels in the United States operates in a climate of fiscal restraint that will persist for the foreseeable future. Added to continuing fiscal constraints are increased public demands for services; political pressures from both inside and outside government; and an often bewildering tangle of laws, judicial rulings, and regulations with which the bureaucracy must contend. Not surprisingly, many of these demands conflict. For example, the bureaucracy has to maintain a measure of distance from society or it risks becoming a tool of a particular interest or class. At the same time, it must represent society or risk undermining public perceptions of its legitimacy. Running through all this is the gravely eroded image of the public service, which is seen by many Americans to be incompetent, unresponsive, unaccountable, and often corrupt. As the Volcker Commission recently reported, the public sector has "been clouded by a sense of frustration inside government and a lack of public trust outside" (National Commission on the Public Service, 1989).

This negative image of the public service is fed by the media, which at times regale the public with vivid and often scathing commentary on incidents of government bungling, waste, red tape, neglect, scandal, and corruption. The media's techniques have become all too familiar; television camera images capturing the plight of the homeless are juxtaposed with reports of a billion-dollar scandal at the U.S. Department of Housing and Urban Development. Added to this are the regular accounts of bureaucratic horror stories, Pentagon waste, a whistle-blower charging public agency misconduct, and highly dramatic incidents such as the recent arrests of New York City teachers on charges of drug sales and child abuse. The list seems endless. These examples of government at its worst offend our moral sensibilities and have helped to create what some observers call a "crisis of legitimacy" for American public administration.

By any objective standards, however, government agencies in the United States function exceedingly well. For example, although it was the target of a recent wave of criticism, this year the Internal Revenue Service will process more than 120 million tax returns. Every month the Social Security Administration distributes payments to millions of the elderly, the poor, and persons with disabilities. And every day across the country the mail is delivered, driving tests are given and licenses are issued, garbage is collected, and countless other essential services are provided to the public. As Charles Goodsell (1983) has argued so convincingly, there is much that is "right" about the bureaucracy.

Justice as a Core Value in Public Administration

This book is about an important aspect of American public administration: administrative justice—what it is, the sources of injustice from which the need for it comes, how government agencies manifest it, and how to achieve it. We begin from the premise James Madison articulated in *Federalist No.*

51: "Justice is the end of government. It is the end of civil society." To fulfill its constitutional responsibilities and to make ours a more just society, American public administration must hold justice to be a paramount concern, not subordinated to political accountability, efficiency and economy, and bureaucratic survival interests. This requires that public administration meet two interrelated obligations: (1) to responsibly implement lawful public policy (to give the people their due) and (2) to deal fairly with people in the process. These twin principles of justice form the nucleus of the administrative justice perspective advanced in the chapters that follow.

As the vignettes at the beginning of the chapter suggest, injustice arises in a variety of administrative settings and appears in many forms. It is often manifested in citizen complaints of government agency abuse or negligence, of failure to monitor agency programs adequately, of violations of personal rights, and of denial of procedures designed to protect individuals. Government agencies are also frequently charged with unfair treatment of their own employees or prospective employees, particularly in performance reviews, merit pay awards, promotion decisions, and hiring decisions.

Clearly, administrators face problems of justice daily, most noticeably when they must allocate benefits or adjudicate disputes, administrative decisions that often call for the exercise of a significant measure of discretion. For example, bureaucratic discretion is exercised daily in judgments on property tax assessments, on which applicants to admit to senior citizen housing, on whom to parole among those incarcerated in prison, on which vendor will be awarded a contract, and on countless other matters. The list of agency actions that have justice implications is virtually endless. Indeed, it is no exaggeration to say that all administrative decision making involves one or more justice issues. The nature and form of the issue will vary from setting to setting, but questions about justice are an inherent and pervasive part of the administrative process.

The case for justice goes well beyond our concerns about specific agency actions to the very nature of public administration in a democratic society. Arguably, the task of organizing any kind of government activity in order to deliver any kind of public good should be viewed as a justice issue. Beginning with the initial policy judgments about the distribution of benefits and burdens among the public, justice issues continue to be manufactured in the countless subsequent decisions made in the course of implementing public policies and programs.

Scholars have called attention to what is termed a "crisis of legitimacy" in American public administration (Freedman, 1978; Harmon and Mayer, 1986). In doing so, they remind us that the authority of any social institution ultimately depends upon popular belief in its legitimacy (Weber, 1947, pp. 130–132). A legislative mandate granting statutory authority to a government agency is by itself insufficient to confer legitimacy upon the agency. The legitimacy of the bureaucracy depends on public perception that it is lawfully carrying out the policies of the regime and serving the core social values of the polity.

The problem of the legitimacy of the bureaucracy can be traced in part to our founding fathers. The federal Constitution nowhere mentions public administration. Because it lacks explicit constitutional status, the bureaucracy encounters recurrent charges that it is usurping constitutional authority. In our constitutional republic, concerned as it must be with fair treatment and participation, commitment to justice as a core value of public administration can promote the public's acceptance of bureaucracy's legitimate role as a constitutional "partner" with the legislative, executive, and judicial branches. The bureaucracy's commitment to justice must include a concern for the quality of administrative processes as well as to the broader distributional justice goals represented in the laws and policies it is required to implement. The legitimacy of the administrative process, in turn, rests on the public's perception that the bureaucracy's decision-making processes are fair. As James O. Freedman expresses it: "It is surprising that more attention has not been given, in the search for sources of administrative legitimacy, to the quality of administrative justice. The procedural rules by which an institution reaches substantive decisions inevitably convey a telling indication of the fairness of its methods, the extent of its interest in protecting individual rights, and the depth of its commitment to attaining just results. In many important respects, the desire and the capacity of government to devise fair procedures for the discharge of its decision-making responsibilities are the essence of democratic practice" (1978, p. 11).

There are compelling reasons for public administration to espouse justice as a core value. The bureaucracy clearly has a general mandate to achieve social justice. As Terry L. Cooper expressed it: "Justice defines the most essential political good; it is the fundamental ordering principle of democratic society from which such goods as political equality, representation of the citizenry, and citizen development are derived" (1987, p. 325).

Justice also is a relatively clear and understandable value that can be employed usefully in administrative practice. It has the virtue of being integrative and can incorporate other values that are important for public administration, such as authority, efficiency, social equity, and the public interest. Finally, and in summation, because justice is a value that has broad social acceptance, its vigorous pursuit can do nothing but lend legitimacy to public administration.

Distinguishing the Various Meanings of Justice

The concept of justice has many meanings. For Aristotle, justice was a human virtue, the "chief of the virtues." He defined injustice, which he took as its mirror opposite, as that which is unjust under the existing moral and legal order, thus equating justice with being law-abiding (Bloom, 1968). This highly conservative view of justice conflicted sharply with that of Plato. The search for Platonic justice coincided with the question of what is the absolute good and, for Plato, this was a political issue. Just action results "when the philosophers, with the help of the warriors, rule over the working class in the same manner in which the individual man arrives at just action by governing his passions with the rational part of the soul . . . " (Kelsen, 1957, p. 104).

Both these conceptions of justice betray individualistic views, as did the views of the utilitarian philosophers Bentham, Mill, and Sidgwick, who believed that justice can be derived from a formula maximizing the total happiness or satisfaction in society (Sterba, 1980, p. 6). It is the same for Kant's categorical imperative, whose formulation requires that we act only on such principles as we wish to be binding on everyone. Since definitions of happiness and universal principles are all the products of our subjective natures, no agreement can be had on how to make these things certain and bring about agreement (Kelsen, 1957).

Yet another unique definition of justice connects it to the concept of efficient distribution of goods. In this view, justice is "an adjustment of relations and ordering of conduct as will make the goods of existence . . . go round as far as possible with the least friction and waste" (Pound, 1959, p. 65). Interestingly, as we will see, this definition has a particular resonance in the history of public administration thought.

John Rawls's concept of justice as fairness also concerns the equitable distribution of the goods of society, particularly the critical positions and practices in its institutions. Rawls was concerned as much with how "moral goods" (such as liberty and human dignity) and "political goods" (for example, power and authority) are distributed as with economic goods. "All social values—liberty and opportunity, income and wealth, and the bases of self-respect—are to be distributed equally unless an unequal distribution of any, or all, of these values is to everyone's advantage" (Rawls, 1971, p. 6). Rawls was especially sensitive to administrative issues, and his work became a major stimulus for the social equity theory movement in academic public administration (Frederickson, 1974; Harmon, 1981, p. 87).

Another sense of the concept is procedural, and this concept has been dominant in the American context. Justice has to do with structuring the rules of decision processes in such ways as to ensure that decision outcomes are unbiased and based on sound data. In this view, the fairness of the procedure causes justice to emerge. For Thomas Jefferson, right procedures meant using democratic process for making the laws, while for Justice Hugo Black it was the operation of a set of primarily judicial safeguards collectively known as procedural due process. The legal profession's traditional view of justice is that it is furthered by using formal, adversarial processes in which each side is represented by competent counsel.

Definitions of justice vary, but they share a common principle: Regardless of which ultimate values are chosen, each person should be given his or her due. All formulations express a view of how to distribute things of value in society, how to punish misdeeds, and how transactions ought to occur—in short, what principles determine a person's due. Defined broadly then, justice may be seen as a set of principles that attach to the decisions, attitudes, and beliefs of individuals, either acting alone or within institutions, both public and private; are widely regarded in a given society as morally correct; are necessary to social functioning; and are used or ought to be used to distribute things of value in society. These "things" are "the conditions and goods that affect individual well-being," where "well-being" broadly includes social, economic, and psychological aspects (Deutsch, 1975, p. 137).

Social justice has dominated the attention of most philosophers who have sought to understand it. Rawls distinguishes social justice from the broader concept of justice in this way: "Many different kinds of things are said to be just and unjust: not only laws, institutions, and social systems, but also particular actions of many kinds, including decisions, judgments, and imputations. We also call the attitudes and dispositions of persons, and persons themselves, just and unjust. Our topic, however, is that of social justice. For us the primary subject of justice is the basic structure of society, or more exactly, the way in which the major social institutions distribute fundamental rights and duties and determine the division of advantages from social cooperation" (1971, p. 7).

The "basic structure of society," of course, includes the political structures and processes of the state. Social justice is served by other social values (for example, constitutionalism, civic duty, freedom of expression), which, in turn, are seen as means to the attainment of the core value. These include dominant societal values and belief patterns, or "regime values," such as those included under the broad rubric of liberty, equality, and property (Rohr, 1978).

Like justice, social justice cannot be defined in absolute terms because to do so would require agreement on ends, on ultimate values. But if ends could be generally agreed upon, could we then arrive at a consensus on the requirements of justice? At least for the subset of those actors known collectively as public administrators within the American state, this seems possible. This group of actors, basically comprising those employed within public agencies and responsible to executive, legislative, and judicial branches, takes an oath to obey the constitutions and the laws of the United States or of the states thereof. Therefore, by virtue of their employment, they declare their ultimate ends to be the legitimate, democratically determined ends sought by the state.

Of course, there is the possibility that specific laws and certain regimes are not themselves legitimated by constitutional and democratic processes. In these cases, the responsibility of public servants to serve the existing government and its policies may not be present. But in normal times, public servants may rely on the general situation that ours is a democratic and pluralistic society that makes its decisions through a pluralistic and representative government, which folds within itself many moral systems and varying definitions of ultimate values.

It follows that justice is made more certain when it is applied more narrowly to the decisions government agencies make. It is possible, therefore, to arrive at a consensus as to what constitutes administrative justice while at the same time being uncertain about what constitutes social justice. Administrative justice is limited to the activities of the government agencies that have as their basic task the carrying out of the broad purposes of public policy. Administrative justice is largely delimited by the distributive policies and decisions flowing from the larger political process. Broad distributive justice policies normally are not determined administratively, and the public can expect that the bureaucracy will accept them as just because they are the product of constitutionally and politically legitimated institutions and practices.

The instruments of distributive policy include the federal and state constitutions, statutes, executive orders, and judicial rulings. Against these, bureaucrats are not free to seek and employ their own personal or idiosyncratic distributive justice preferences but usually are bound by duty to implement lawful distributive policies, even when they may disagree with a policy or find it personally distasteful. This is not to say that administrators must implement policy blindly, for there are times when justice requires that the administrator act contrary to a law, policy, or rule.

In the real world, of course, agency administrators are important political players. They mobilize political support for new programs or the continuation of old ones (Long, 1949). They work closely with executive office officials, legislative committee staff, and others directly engaged in public policymaking. Thus they have a proper and important role to play in bringing their expertise and special knowledge, and values, to bear in making law, in preventing the original formulation or reauthorization of unjust policies. Yet, once those laws and policies are in place, the responsibility of the bureaucracy to effectively bring these policies to fruition is clear.

Administrative justice is distinguished from the broader concepts of justice and social justice by the constitutional-legal arrangements, laws, regime values, and specific roles that attach to bureaucratic positions and authority. Administrative justice is thus unique to public administration. Its function is to help bureaucracy serve the ends of social justice through generally accepted and legitimated practices sanctioned by dominant regime values. That is, when the bureaucracy acts in pursuit of social justice goals, justice requires that it do so by means that are themselves recognized as fair and just. From such reasoning comes the basic tenet of justice: to give one his or her due, realized within the realm of administrative activity.

The Search for a Normative Base
for Public Administration

Given the compelling case that justice is, or ought to be, a fundamental imperative for administrative agencies, it is surprising that the concept has not received greater attention as a central normative premise for American public administration. Why is it that the public administration community has not embraced justice more wholeheartedly and articulated its requirements?

The answer to this question is complex. It lies in part in the attraction that other normative premises have held for the field, particularly the powerful lure of concepts such as the public interest and social equity and the dominating influence of the twin values of efficiency and economy. It also lies in the historical conflict between public administration and the legal profession, which includes the erroneous assumption made by many that justice concerns are best left to the lawyers and the courts.

Consider first the matter of competing normative premises. All administrative decisions fundamentally involve making a choice or judgment with regard to some norm, standard, or value. Thus values are a vital element in administrative decision making and no decision process is ever value free or completely neutral. The basic question for public administration is: What values or normative premises should serve as the basis for decision making?

In the private sector, decision making typically is based on "the profit motive." Depending on the decision context, the term "profit" may take on any of a number of meanings, such as return on investment or net income. Of course, business decisions may involve considerations other than profit making, such as social responsibility or market share. Still, profit making is a clear and powerful value in the private sector that continues to be the dominant normative premise for business decision making. "Good" business decisions are decisions that further the firm's goal of profitability.

There is no similar consensus on the appropriate normative grounds for decision making in the public sector, due in large measure to the continuing debate over the role of public administration in American society. The debate has taken many forms, centering on several related core issues: (1) the proper role of bureaucratic authority in a democratic society, having to do with administrative responsibility and accountability and the boundaries to be placed on administrative discretion; (2) the utility of the concept of the public interest; (3) the meaning and limits of rationality in organizational decision making; and (4) the relative importance that should be attached to efficiency or "technical rationality" in public administration.

The lack of consensus on these issues is hardly surprising, given their complexity and the diversity of viewpoints expressed by leading scholars (see Harmon and Mayer, 1986). The difficulty in identifying for public administration a viable counterpart to the business world's concept of "profit" is illustrated in the sharply contrasting assessments of the utility—or vacuity—of one of the most important and widely debated concepts in the field: efficiency.

Efficiency as a Decision Premise. From Woodrow Wilson's now famous essay in 1887 calling for the separation of administration from politics through much of contemporary writing on organizational productivity, observers of both public- and private-sector organizations have preached the gospel of efficiency as a kind of secular religion in American society.

The rational model of bureaucracy, with its emphasis on efficiency, continues to exert a profound influence on thinking about public organizations. Robert Denhardt argues that "the use of technical rationality (often translated as 'efficiency') as the main criteria for evaluating organization life remain(s) at the core of thinking about public organizations" (Denhardt, 1984, p. 89). In fact, it is not an exaggeration to say that our thinking about public administration in terms of efficiency (or technical rationality) is so deeply rooted that it is difficult even to think about managing public organizations in alternative terms. As Dwight Waldo tells us: "[N]ot only is the classical theory still today the formal working theory of large numbers of persons technically concerned with administrative-organizational matters, both in the public and private spheres, but I expect it will be around a long, long time . . . a social theory widely held by the actors has a self-confirming tendency and the classical theory is now deeply ingrained in our culture" (1961, p. 220).

In his classic essay, *The Administrative State,* Waldo (1948) first challenged the maxim of efficiency. He argued that efficiency is hardly the "impartial" or "scientific" value that scientific management and classical theorists made it out to be (Taylor, 1947; Gulick, 1937). On the contrary, argued Waldo, efficiency is a slippery concept, too vague to serve as a primary value. Things are not simply "efficient" or "inefficient," he noted. "They are efficient or inefficient for given purposes, and efficiency for one purpose may mean inefficiency for another" (Waldo, 1948, p. 202).

Whether something is efficient or not depends on what objectives are sought. For example, it may well be quicker and less costly for an agency to purchase a new computer system without having to follow procurement requirements that often are quite cumbersome. But to the extent that public accountability is an important concern, then the formal procurement process may indeed be an efficient means to achieve that end.

In contrast to justice, efficiency is important as an instrumental value rather than an end in itself. As such, the search for efficiency inevitably involves other important ends or values. Instead of treating efficiency as an end value, therefore, it is important to ask: efficiency for what purpose? What other ends or values are being sought? Parole officers may arrange their schedules to maximize the number of parolees seen daily, but does mere visitation alter their behavior toward less criminal activity?

The concept of efficiency is borrowed from economics and is best understood in terms analogous to business (Chandler, 1987). Although the concept is based on observation of large complex organizations, the private sector differs from the public sector in several important ways, including profit motive, the concentration of labor, competition, differing social expectations of employee behavior, managerial freedom in personnel matters, structuring of authority, political and amateur leadership in government, and the complexity of goals (Chandler, 1987, pp. 580–586). Add to these differences the requirements of openness and the use of mandated, democratic procedures and both the tasks and goals of managing in the public sector become wholly different from those in the private sector. Chandler concludes: "Given all these purposes of government employment which have little to do with management efficiency and which even militate against it, the criterion of efficiency appears to be misplaced in the extent to which it is used to evaluate the effectiveness of American public administration" (1987, p. 586).

The inappropriateness of efficiency as *the* central normative premise for public administration has been widely acknowledged in academic public administration, but the search for an alternative paradigm has not been successful (Marini, 1971; Harmon and Mayer, 1986). Efforts to develop a normative-prescriptive theory of public administration based on values such as the public interest and social equity have been fruitful but have failed to displace technical rationality as the dominant paradigm of the field.

The Public Interest. At first blush, the concept of the public interest has great intuitive appeal as a normative premise for public administration. After all, public administrators are engaged in implementing laws, policies, and programs adopted in the name of the public and requiring the use of public resources. They are therefore expected to

use these resources to bring about socially favorable outcomes. To justify an action as being in the public interest,
it must "serve the ends of the whole public rather than
those of some sector of the public," at least in the long run
(Meyerson and Banfield, 1955, p. 322). Thus some concept
of the public interest surely must guide public administrators' decision making. But is there such a thing as a common concept of the public interest? And if there is, what
does it mean when applied to specific administrative decisions? Public administration theorists have debated these
questions for decades without resolution.

Many prominent scholars consider the concept of the
public interest to be much too vague to have any practical
utility for public administrators (for example, Miewald, 1978;
Schubert, 1960; Sorauf, 1962). To be sure, the concept also
has its advocates. Bailey believes that the public interest "is
the central concept of a civilized society" (1962, p. 106).
Herring said that the concept of the public interest is to
bureaucracy what the due process clause is to the judiciary
(1936, p. 23). For its supporters, the importance of the public
interest does not lie in its precision as an analytical construct
but rather in its focus on public accountability and responsibility for administrative officials. Just and responsible public
administrators, it is argued, will act in the public interest.

Although it is true that we are not likely to succeed in
defining the public interest successfully in the abstract, its
meaning may come into sharper focus as we encounter specific decision problems, for example, in areas involving public
health and safety. Is it in the public interest for a state environmental protection agency to permit a chemical company
to dump toxic wastes into a stream that flows past its plant?
Or for the head of a city public works department to award
contracts to friends? These are starkly drawn examples, but
they suggest that, although the precise determination of the
public interest may not be possible, it nonetheless is possible
to distinguish the broad boundaries of public versus private
interests. If this is true, the problem lies less in the impreci-
sion of the concept of the public interest than in the need for

a set of standards or criteria for rationally making decision choices that are in the public interest.

Social Equity. John Rawls's formulation of the meaning of social justice as fairness prescribes a more equitable distribution of the goods of society, most particularly the critical positions and practices in its institutions. Decisions regarding the distribution of benefits within social institutions are just when in accord with certain principles dictating that all persons benefit and that the liberties of no one are sacrificed for the benefit of others (Rawls, 1971, pp. 75–83). Rawls was particularly sensitive to administrative issues, and his work became a major stimulus for the social equity movement in public administration (Harmon, 1981, p. 87).

Heralded at first as the cornerstone of a "new public administration," this promising initiative never fully blossomed. Nonetheless, the sentiment for the achievement of social equity continues in the ongoing work of public administration scholars (Frederickson, 1990, for example). It is based on egalitarian principles and is concerned with the public administrator's role in bringing about a more equitable distribution of public benefits and government jobs.

The social equity approach assumes that public administrators are not and should not be value-neutral. The delivery of public services typically varies depending on the recipient's social, economic, and political status—the higher the status, the better the service. The public administrator is morally obligated to counter this tendency by making decisions in the direction of providing greater equity in service delivery. Variations from equity should always be in the direction of more services to the disadvantaged. Finally, public administrators must be proactive, because "the isolation of administrators and public agencies from either political or administrative responsibility is not equity enhancing" (Frederickson, 1971, p. 3).

Social equity theory places a strong value on accomplishing goals such as effective police protection, education, and defense for *all* citizens, including the poor and powerless.

Such an equity ethic is needed to balance interests that seek to promote efficiency, economy, and professional or career responsibilities.

Justice Preempted or Justice Abandoned?

The Former Role of the Bureaucracy in Providing Justice. American public administration has not embraced justice as a core value, which in the current era may be due in large part to the dominant influence the legal profession and legal norms have come to have in administrative decision making. But in an earlier time, during the 1940s and 1950s, the courts showed considerable deference to the bureaucracy on matters within the latter's zone of expertise. Judges were unwilling to substitute their judgment for the bureaucracy's on policy matters, even when issues of justice and fair treatment were involved (Shapiro, 1988). Even when mandating procedural protections available to persons subject to administrative action, the courts often gave the bureaucracy wide latitude to determine the best ways to meet constitutional responsibilities. Because of this judicial deference, the bureaucracy in the past was accorded a significant role and the opportunity to serve as a guarantor of justice. That it often failed in that role seems clear (Rosenbloom, 1983a).

Since that time, increasing "judicialization" of the administrative decision process has taken place. This trend is somewhat of a paradox and reflects the declining confidence of the courts and other lawmakers in the bureaucracy's ability to deliver justice; it also probably mirrors public attitudes. It is enhanced by the deference that academic and practicing public administration have paid to the legal profession and the courts on matters of justice. Instead of carving out a meaningful role as a legitimate partner with the courts in acting as a guarantor of justice, public administration has had a largely reactive posture, responding to external demands and taking its guidance from the courts and the legal profession.

By failing to fully develop the role of guarantor of justice, public administration has neglected its responsibility to serve justice. Moreover, it has squandered a unique opportunity to achieve public legitimacy. This is not to say that all, or even most, public agencies and public administrators are unconcerned about justice: Certainly there are countless public servants who have a strong commitment to justice principles. It simply means that, faced with multiple and conflicting demands, public organizations have tended to hold to technical rationality, political accountability, and bureaucratic survival as dominant values.

The Dominance of the Legal Profession. Beginning in the 1930s, the legal profession pressed its claim to a dominant role in the "business of doing justice" in government agencies. There is a powerful professional drive to keep adjudicatory decision making out of the hands of the bureaucrats, particularly where the decisions affect private interests.

Moreover, the legal profession's particular views of what constitutes administrative justice and the limited role of the bureaucracy within it have in the main been accepted by the American public, including the bureaucracy itself. Whenever the legal profession has exerted its influence to define justice standards for the bureaucracy, the public administration community has responded with timidity and deference.

To compound the problem, the development of the academic study of public administration has supported the dominance of administrative justice by the legal profession. Perhaps most important, public administration study increasingly has taken on a narrowly focused view of the field, concerned more with technical management issues than with constitutional-legal and political aspects. This academic bias is well established and deeply rooted. For example, in the first major American textbook on public administration, Leonard White said what was popularly believed at the time and represents what many still hold to be true, that "the study of administration should start from the base of management rather than the foundation of law, and is therefore more absorbed in the affairs of the American Management Association than in the decisions of the courts" (1926, pp. vii–viii).

The emergence of the legal profession's dominance of administrative justice can be seen in the evolution of the study of administrative law in the United States. In the 1930s, when administrative law began to be taught in American colleges and universities, it was offered to combined classes of law and public administration students, in a way that blurred any differentiation in the specific interests of the two groups. A sharing of scholarship and an interchange of faculty occurred that was not too dissimilar from the traditional continental practice of teaching public administration and administrative law as an integrated subject.

The combined legal-political-administrative approach to administrative law was short-lived. Beginning in the 1940s, law schools began to teach the subject with casebooks composed almost entirely of appellate court opinions. The subject matter was concentrated almost entirely upon regulation and private rights and was far more concerned with what courts do than with what agencies do. Within public administration programs, administrative law came to be regarded as a rather specialized field and was often "farmed out" to lawyers to teach, when it was taught at all (Dimock, 1980, pp. 68–69).

One can easily demonstrate the continuing and pervasive appeal and influence of this administration-law dichotomy in academic public administration. All one needs to do is survey any standard textbook on the subject, scan the tables of contents of recent issues of leading journals in the field, or examine the curriculum of a typical master's degree program in public administration. One finds that surprisingly little attention is given to justice as a central responsibility for public administration and that the treatment of administrative justice issues typically occurs in the context of administrative law. Even when administrative justice is treated, it is with the view that bureaucrats either must become more "lawyerlike" or yield to the expertise of the legal profession in such matters.

Justice is not normally seen as a pervasive activity of

administrative agencies. Many nonlawyers will argue that justice is only an important concern of *some* public agencies,
such as law enforcement agencies, and is not central to the
primary mission or operations of most agencies. In the same
vein, justice is seen to be a specific task belonging to specialized units of the agency, such as hearings and appeals and
equal employment opportunity offices. In the mainstream
view, justice is a specialized function within the domain of
public administration.

Alternatively, lawyers and judges tend to see administrative justice concerned only with agency rule making and
formal adjudication within the agencies and with the judicial
review of such activities, a view that confuses administrative
justice with administrative law. The two are by no means
synonymous. Administrative justice has to do with far more
than judicial control and formal procedure: It applies to the
vast range of bureaucratic decision making in every public
agency at each level of government.

Achieving administrative justice requires that public
administrators reclaim justice as a core value, equal to or
greater in weight than technical rationality, political accountability, and bureaucratic survival. One thing is certain: The
achievement of administrative justice cannot be left only to
the courts, the legal profession, or specialized units in government agencies. Justice should be everybody's business.

The Injustice Perspective

As Judith Shklar (1990) tells us, justice and injustice are not
polar opposites. Justice is the stuff of philosophy and theol-
ogy. Discussions about it are cerebral, abstract, and rational.
When a government system or policy is just, it is taken for
granted and attracts little notice. On the other hand, injustice
is personal, particular in its application, and intensely felt by
those who suffer it. Plays are written about it; revolutions are
fought over it; history is written about its effects. The direct
results of injustice are vengeful acts and the escalation of
conflict or, all too often, a degrading acceptance of one's polit-

ical impotence. Injustice is emotional and requires little analysis; we know it when we feel it.

Injustice is not simply the result of the breakdown of the primary justice system. Conversely, procedures and rules seeking justice are provided in response to the recognition of injustice. Moreover, they cannot by themselves erase the injustice. This is so for political and psychological reasons. Inequalities are inherent in our society, and to a greater or lesser degree the political system will reflect them. Also, because injustice has a strong psychological component (that is, the injustice is associated with anger, a desire for vengeance, or shame), even where the government's response is designed to right the injustice, it will normally fall short of eliminating the psychological damage. Only revenge might do that, but the government cannot allow revenge without sanctioning more injustice and escalating social discontent and conflict.

The sense of injustice arises from a violation by another of an expectation, as occurs when a promise is broken or when people feel deprived of something they believe they are entitled to. It has enormous psychological force, is universal, and is instinctive in human beings.

What all this means for public administration is that somehow public organizations must come to grips with the psychological aspects of injustice, or the benefits accruing from making just decisions will be partially undermined. This does not mean that the bureaucracy has the duty of *preventing* injustice to its citizens; indeed, such an achievement is a political impossibility. It does mean that public administrators must give voice to the sense of outrage that many individuals and groups inevitably experience to mitigate loss of dignity and efficacy and to conduct themselves in a manner that avoids further inflaming the sense of injustice.

Implications of the Administrative Justice Perspective

What does the responsibility for administrative justice (serving legitimate policy ends by means that treat people fairly) mean for public administration in a constitutional democracy?

First, it means recognizing that there are limits to the broad use of discretionary authority by the bureaucracy. Public administrators do far more than merely concern themselves with the efficient implementation of public policy. They play an important role in policymaking and in building and maintaining support for government programs. And very often they act in a judicial capacity, such as when they hear and settle disputes. To be accepted as legitimate constitutional partners, however, they must justify their exercise of broad discretionary power.

This can be difficult, both because the bureaucracy lacks explicit constitutional status and because the public fears and mistrusts a powerful bureaucracy. When public administrators shape governmental policy and adjudicate disputes, many may see them as exceeding their proper authority and violating the doctrine of separation of powers.

A commitment to justice can do much to fill the "legitimacy gap" facing American public administration. First, as a preeminent social value, justice may be said to underlie our constitutional system. Indeed, our country's founding revolution was rooted in important part in the demand for justice. The rationale for the Declaration of Independence is the list of injustices visited on the colonies by the British crown. The Constitution seeks to ensure the gains of the revolution, proclaiming in the preamble that a major purpose of the fundamental law of the country shall be to "establish justice."

Second, serving the ends of justice means that, in order to fulfill their legitimate constitutional role in the political system, bureaucrats must accept personal responsibility for their discretionary actions. In order to honor the lawgiver's purpose, they must be proactive in determining the meaning of the laws they implement and the policy principles underlying them. Conflict in the interpretation of laws is inevitable, for legislation often is ambiguous, either intentionally as part of a political compromise or because of the inherent uncertainty of language. Sometimes, laws enacted to achieve certain purposes are poorly designed. Government policies and programs often run into unanticipated problems of implementation. In all of these cases, administrators imbued with a concept of justice have the responsibility to seek correction of the law, or to find lawful means of fulfilling the policy objectives of the lawmakers (Burke, 1986). And, as we have already noted, at times justice may require that the public administrator act contrary to the law, policy, or rule—and be prepared to be held accountable.

A special, dramatic circumstance of the need for a proactive public administration is that of the unjust regime. Consider the case of the decent, honorable professional serving in the public service of a Nazi-occupied country in World War II. When the Nazis occupied Denmark in 1943, the German governor decreed that any Jews living in Denmark were to be identified preparatory to the confiscation of their property, their detention, and their probable extermination. The Danish bureaucracy resisted and refused to be the instrument of the Nazi conquerors (Frederickson and Hart, 1985).

Contrast this to the behavior of the Vichy government in France during the Nazi occupation, where civil servants abetted and even ordered the deportation of children to extermination camps in 1944. Undoubtedly, some Vichy officials cooperated with the Nazis out of ambition, greed, anti-Semitism, and, of course, fear. But were not these same forces (at least potentially) acting in Denmark as well? And yet the Danish civil service resisted the might of the Third Reich. They acted not upon the occupier's law, or the dictates of efficiency, or duty to the hierarchy, but upon the requirements of justice.

Finally, a commitment to administrative justice requires the acceptance of change. Administrative agencies have developed structures, behaviors, decision routines, and operating procedures appropriate to the needs of politics and efficiency and their own peculiar cultures, and not explicitly or even implicitly to pursue the end of justice. In order to allow the value of justice to gain currency in public organizations, much change will be necessary: in the structural designs of organizations; in how they interact with the public; in the criteria they must take into account in their decision processes; in the way they recruit, select, reward, promote, and train; right down to the attitudes they inculcate in their personnel. Much of the balance of this book deals with these matters.

2

ADMINISTRATIVE JUSTICE AS ADMINISTRATIVE LAW: THE TRADITIONAL VIEW

If a new vision of a just public administration is to be pursued, it is important to understand what administrative justice has meant in the past, how it has been defined and practiced, and how it has evolved. In this chapter we will concentrate upon the single most important source of administrative justice.

Administrative law and the legal profession have played a crucial role in determining how administrative agencies at all levels of government perceive and act upon notions of justice. Law has shaped the prevailing values, forms, and behaviors relative to justice. If public administration is to reclaim justice, it is first necessary to know something of this history and how and why so much of the field of public administration has come to be judicialized.

The Relationship Between Administrative Justice and Administrative Law

Administrative law, according to Kenneth Culp Davis, is "the law concerning the powers and procedures of administrative agencies, including especially the law governing judicial review of administrative action" (1975, p. 6). A considerable gap exists between the range of administrative decisions subject to administrative law and the much larger spectrum of decisions that public agencies make. Administrative law is constrained in several ways.

First, it relates more to procedure and remedies than to substantive law, more to the law controlling administrative agencies than to the law produced by them. For example, in a proceeding before a state environmental protection agency to consider better methods to dispose of hazardous wastes, administrative law applies to such matters as who may testify, what evidence may be introduced, and on what basis a court may review whatever decision emerges, whereas the decision relating to how waste is to be disposed of is not itself a subject.

Second, administrative law relates to and grows out of the clash between public action and private interests, and it usually attempts to protect the latter. It "is based upon the assumption that administrative discretion should be constrained primarily to protect the private rights of those subject to administrative power" (Bryner, 1987, p. 34).

Third, many of its practitioners would confine its application to two primary types of agencies: regulatory agencies and agencies that administer benefits programs. Although the federal Administrative Procedure Act (APA) defines "agency" to include executive branch agencies generally, Schwartz feels the definition is too inclusive. "The administrative lawyer is not concerned with every agency exercising executive powers. His concern is primarily with those aspects of administrative authority that affect private rights and obligations" (1976, pp. 3-4). Not to be included, says Schwartz, are agencies or parts of agencies concerned with defense and foreign affairs or internal "housekeeping" functions (such as the General Services Administration or Office of Personnel Management); those that are engaged solely in planning, fact gathering, or making studies; and other agencies that operate public services that were formerly private.

A final limitation of administrative law is that it relates to both rulemaking and adjudication that take place in more formalized hearing settings. It excludes such things as internal agency management policy and the type of informal dispute settlement that goes on routinely in administrative offices. Davis estimates that the procedural safeguards and judicial review processes of administrative law are largely irrelevant to 90 percent of agency decisions (Davis, 1975).

Despite the fact that administrative law deals only partially with the kinds of decisions made by public administrators, the legal profession tends toward the view that it constitutes the whole of administrative justice. Furthermore, the profession has been successful in convincing many non-lawyers, including many public administrators, that its view is correct. To the conventional legal mind, the problem of administrative justice is one of making administrative decisions conform to superior political authority and subjecting administrative procedures to certain safeguards familiar to the legal profession in the courtroom. Most fundamentally, the problem is seen as properly protecting private rights of clients against the abuse of governmental power.

The "problem of administrative law," whether it be one of taming the administrative state to conform to superior authority, guaranteeing procedural fairness, or protecting private rights and interests, is seen by most of us, not just lawyers, as requiring the use of methods and norms common to the legal profession. Administrative decisions to be scrutinized are those characterized as "rulemaking," "adjudication," or "enforcement," and they do not include the informal decisions that constitute what many legal and political scholars acknowledge to be the lifeblood of administrative decision making. No court or legislative body or executive will review the great bulk of administrative decisions; these decisions will depend, for the achievement of justice, upon the routines and values established by public administrators themselves.

The Influence of Law on Administrative Justice

If we are to understand the role of law in administrative justice systems in federal and state governments in the United States, it is necessary to turn to history. What forces have favored the legal profession in its battle to gain dominance vis-à-vis public administration in administrative dispute settlement and administrative policymaking? How has administrative law developed? What are the trends and current directions of administrative law, and how are they likely to influence the decision behavior of administrative agencies?

Pre-New Deal. Administrative law, although well developed on the European continent, was a relatively unknown subject in the United States before the 1930s. This state of affairs was due in large measure to the American doctrines of the rule of law and the separation of powers. The rule of law, associated with the legal philosophy of Alfred Dicey, dictated that government be treated like any litigant by the regular courts and be subject to the same provisions of law as any individual. There were no specialized public or administrative law forums such as those on the continent (Shapiro, 1988). The courts and the Constitution, not the government, were viewed as the guardians of the public interest. The separation of powers doctrine and nondelegation doctrines forbade both the grant to and the combination of powers within agencies. These views dominated American legal thought in the early part of the twentieth century.

Despite the antagonism of the legal profession, American governments continued to increase administrative power. Hearing examiners, the prototype of modern administrative law judges, were created in various American administrative agencies dating back to the early nineteenth century. The practice of delegating hearing duties to single administrative officials has its roots in the practice of the British Court of Chancery. The pattern was copied in the United States, beginning in 1812, with registers of the General Land Office who settled disputes involving the sale of public lands. It was repeated with the empowerment of local inspectors with investigative and hearing duties in connection with ship safety and supervision of merchant marine personnel, starting in 1838. The Interstate Commerce Commission established hearing examiners in the first decade of the twentieth century, and a number of other federal and state agencies followed this general pattern (Musolf, 1953, pp. 47–74).

The New Deal. The "sudden, enormous, and politically controversial expansion of the federal bureaucracy by the New Deal . . . led to a crucial reevaluation of the Diceyan tradition that had dominated American legal thought" (Shapiro, 1988, p. 38). Roosevelt and the Congress created scores of new government programs, armed with a bewildering diversity of experimental investigative and hearing techniques. The New Dealers' interest in social change made them less tolerant of private property rights protection than the courts or the legal profession. According to Nonet, "the architects of the welfare state had a characteristically narrow and negative conception of the role of law in government. To them, law evoked a system of rigid constraints that paralyzed initiative and prevented effective action to solve the problems of society. Government had to be freed from undue legalism, relieved of the burdensome formalism of legal procedure" (1969, p. 3).

These views alarmed the legal profession. The role of the hearing examiner became a major battleground in the ideological fight between the progressive forces of New Deal liberalism and the politically conservative, private interest-oriented forces represented by the American Bar Association (ABA). For many lawyers, administrative procedural experimentation marked "a shocking deviation from common-law standards of justice" (Musolf, 1953, p. 30). The ABA's Special Committee on Administrative Law concluded that administrative decision procedures had to be regularized and standards developed that could then serve as a basis for judicial review of agency decisions (Cooper, 1983, p. 75).

The climactic battle was fought over the passage of the Walter-Logan bill in 1939. In his veto of the bill, which contained the ABA's formula for subjecting almost all administrative policymaking to legal process and judicial review (Musolf, 1953, pp. 41–42), President Roosevelt spoke for public administration when he said the measure was "one of the repeated efforts by a combination of lawyers who desire to have all processes of government conducted through lawsuits and of interests which desire to escape regulation. . . ." He complained that "a large part of the legal profession has never reconciled itself to the existence of the administrative tribunal. Many of them prefer the stately ritual of courts, in which lawyers play all the speaking parts, to the simple procedure of administrative hearings which a client can understand and even participate in" (Roosevelt, 1939, pp. 2–3).

The APA and the Period of Compromise. Although Roosevelt successfully vetoed the legal profession's attempt to legislate a statutory administrative law, he asked the attorney general to appoint a committee to investigate the need for reform (Davis, 1975, p. 12). The resulting Attorney General's Committee on Administrative Procedure, a group of respected legal scholars and administrative leaders, recommended a modest statutory framework that prescribed procedures for rulemaking, adjudication, and judicial review and determined methods for the selection and protection of hearing officers from agency influence (U.S. Congress, 1946, p. 6). Their work led to the passage of the federal Administrative Procedure Act of 1946 (the APA). The APA accepts the principle that diverse agency practices are proper and are not to be regulated by a single, simple set of uniform rules. However, it provides a residual back-up function. "Where the particular statute creating a government agency or a specific government program did not specify how the agency was to do certain things, then the agency was to look to the general provisions of the APA" (Shapiro, 1988, p. 39).

According to Bryner (1987, pp. 30–31), the APA rested on a number of assumptions.

1. The administrative process it creates is a justice system designed to protect the rights of individuals affected by administrative actions and to limit administrative discretion.
2. The courts serve as the major safeguard against the abuse of administrative power through litigation brought by persons aggrieved by agency actions.

3. Formal case-by-case adjudication is the most important form of administrative action.
4. Congress maintains oversight.

The enactment of the APA represented a compromise between the legal profession and public administration and ushered in a period of uneasy reconciliation between the two. The federal judiciary came to tolerate administrative power and to defer to the elective branches and to agency expertise and discretion (Cooper, 1983; Rosenbloom, 1983a, p. 56). The pattern was repeated at the state level with the promulgation by the National Conference of Commissioners on Uniform State Laws of a Model State Administrative Procedure Act, which has been used as a basis to regularize adjudication, rulemaking, and judicial review in most states (Davis, 1975, p. 13).

Although there is great diversity among the states, the principal features of the APAs (both federal and state) are these:

- Hearing examiners (also called administrative law judges, hearing officers, or referees) are established as semiautonomous agents with responsibilities for both rulemaking and adjudication. They are to be insulated from other agency decision makers, off-the-record communication, and prosecutory personnel.
- Formal adjudication is conducted in the agency under those circumstances where the legislation creating the agency expressly requires the agency to hold hearings.
- Informal rulemaking is conducted, in which agencies issue rules and regulations after giving public notice and allowing the public to make comment (also called "notice and comment" proceedings).
- The right of aggrieved parties to judicial review is liberally observed.

In both federal and state governments, most administrative decisions are not affected by the decision-making procedures of APAs. First, as already noted, statutes creating the agencies or specific programs may provide for special procedures, which must then be followed. Second, APAs exclude informal decisions from their operation. To the lawyer and within the meaning of the act, an agency acts informally when it is neither making rules nor holding formal hearings.

Judicialization of Administrative Processes. The compromise upon which the APAs were built collapsed in the 1960s. The rise in the activities and the power of the administrative state prompted reaction from each of the three political branches of government (Carroll, 1982; Rourke, 1987; Rosenbloom, 1983a, pp. 28-30). State legislatures, for example, have used periodic "sunset review" to assess whether agency performance has furthered legislated goals. About twenty states use a rulemaking review process, which requires a legislative body to pass judgment upon administrative rules before they can be considered to be legally effective. In some states, the executive exercises a rulemaking clearance function to approve or disapprove rules and regulations before they become effective. Judicialization is a consequence of the rise of the administrative state and the resulting reaction of the courts and the legal profession to bureaucratic power. Their response insisted on a showing of bureaucratic accountability in ways that the legal profession can understand and control. The federal judiciary began to actively restrict administrative power after Earl Warren was sworn in as chief justice. Thus was ushered in an era of democratization, in which the courts, both federal and state, sought to increase the voice of many groups in the administrative process, including those who were impoverished, incapacitated, or institutionalized. It was also an era in which the courts created a great deal of new administrative law.

The hallmark of the Warren era was the judicialization of many of the decision processes of administrative agencies, at all levels of government. As L. A. Smith said: "The 'judicialization of the administrative process' is a phrase descriptive of several related phenomena. It is probably used most often to refer to active participation of the courts, through extensive judicial review, in the decisions of executive bodies. But it can also refer to the expanding use of trial-like procedures for making governmental decisions, and more generally, to overproceduralization and excessive complexity in the process of making public policy decisions" (1985, p. 428).

Standards for judicially structuring administrative decision processes during this era were sought through an expansive interpretation of federal and state administrative procedure acts and of the due process clauses of the Fifth and Fourteenth Amendments to the federal Constitution. The influence of the federal judiciary permeated the state judiciaries as well, and so judicialization was as much a feature of state administrative decision processes as it was of federal administrative decision processes.

The beneficiaries of the expansion of procedural rights in the agencies included individual citizens, corporate entities, government employees, and, importantly, the disadvantaged and racial minorities. Most notably for our purposes, the Warren court stressed the participation of all groups and their legal representatives in the decision-making processes of the agencies. A list of the significant changes wrought during these years would include

1. The articulation of new and expanded *substantive* constitutional rights and liberties, such as the right of government employees and prison inmates to privacy. These rights were to be implemented and enforced in administrative settings.
2. An expansion in the number of those agency hearings that were subject to the general constitutional safeguards of "administrative due process," to settle a vast range of disputes (well beyond those defined by the various APAs).
3. A bias for adjudication over rulemaking, at least in federal government agencies. This preference was buttressed by legislation, particularly in the 1970s, requiring adversarial, trial-type procedures in administrative rulemaking (Bryner, 1987, pp. 27–29; Cooper, 1988, pp. 129–134).
4. The erosion of the immunity of governments and their

officials from suit by members of the public. The fashioning of a new public official liability law caused administrators to become increasingly cautious and to look to their legal advisers for guidance in policymaking and implementation strategies.

5. The occasional taking over by courts of the management of public institutions (Horowitz, 1983; Gilmour, 1982). A famous example is the running of the Boston school system by a federal district court.

6. The growth of participation in administrative decision processes by cause-based public interest groups that protected various consumer, special interest, and citizen groups (Reagan, 1987, pp. 93–95). This development went hand in hand with new judicial rules permitting greater citizen access to the courts and legislative provisions giving fee incentives to lawyers to take class actions.

In this period there was rapid growth of constitutional law relating to administrative agencies, with movement away from the APA as the focus of administrative justice. The administrative "due process explosion" grew directly out of the courts' reading of what "fundamental fairness" required in administrative decision settings. The courts' answers to that question greatly expanded the number of decision makers responsible for dispute settlement as well as the kinds of decisions that were subject to judicial review. Prison wardens, school principals, welfare and health officials, and many others were held accountable to due process standards when they made decisions that had the potential of depriving persons of life, liberty, or property.

Although growing in volume, the rulemaking responsibilities of administrative agencies were increasingly subjected to court-style constraints. "Old-style" regulation, which stressed the making of economic policy by regulatory agencies within broad discretionary powers given to them by legislatures, gave way to "new-style" regulation in the 1960s and early 1970s. New-style regulation focused on social and health-oriented agencies operating under tighter legislative guidelines that reduced administrative discretion and increased judicial review. "[T]he new social legislation became extremely specific, including details that even the most sympathetic observer finds surprising as matters to be embedded in legislation, rather than left to administrative discretion" (Reagan, 1987, pp. 95–98). Within this environment, the courts required rulemakers to respond to all issues raised by participating parties, including trivial ones, to build a "rule-making record," and to state reasons for their decisions (Shapiro, 1988, pp. 44–49).

These moves by the courts appear to be responses to sharply rising demands for representation and rights in the administrative state, coming from black, Hispanic, women's, environmental, and other underrepresented or special interest groups. The courts responded by fashioning an administrative law according to an interest representation model (Stewart, 1975; Garland, 1985). The core of the model is the belief that underrepresentation of the powerless is the major problem in the administrative decision process, and increased participation is the cure. Acting on this assumption, the courts proceeded to liberalize access to administrative forums, to require more trial-type hearings to ensure to all groups full opportunity to assert their interests, and to increase judicial scrutiny of administrative actions to make sure that agencies were in fact conforming to new judicial guidelines concerning access and judicialized procedure. The focus was on getting a politically balanced resolution of disputes in the agency, using the latter as a "surrogate legislature" (Garland, 1985, pp. 510–511).

No development more typifies the Warren era than the series of decisions that brought about the huge expansion in the frequency of formal agency hearings. The most notable case was *Goldberg v. Kelly* (1970), where a majority of the Court held that hearings, with specific and formalized procedural safeguards, must be offered to persons before terminating public assistance payments. The courts adopted hearing requirements, with varying degrees of formality, for disputes arising in prisons, mental hospitals, schools, and other places

where persons alleged that the government was threatening
property, liberty, or life.

As a result of these judicial actions, public administrators were compelled to observe the constitutionally protected
rights of a wide variety of groups and individuals, many of
whom previously had been excluded from administrative adjudicative processes. Together with rights extended by state and
federal legislation and executive action relating to such matters as racial and sex discrimination in employment, collective
bargaining rights, equal pay for men and women for equal
work, freedom of information, and workplace safety, these
court-created rights constituted an important part of an expanding social justice for many in the political system as a
whole.

The courts put pressure on administrators to comply
with the new requirements by making them, personally, and
their employing agencies vulnerable to liability by lawsuit.
Both the Warren and early Burger courts extended such liability to damages resulting from depriving any person (even a
noncitizen) of rights granted by federal law. In *Wood v. Strickland* (1975), the Court said that school board officials were
liable for acts which they or their agents knew or "reasonably
should have known" would violate a person's constitutional
rights. This was an exceptionally significant expansion of
public official liability for public administrators, as before
that time they enjoyed a qualified immunity from liability.

In this period also the public interest law firm emerged
in response to the courts' creation of the "public law litigation model" (Chayes, 1976). Formed by socially and politically
conscious private-sector lawyers to represent the disadvantaged, environmentalist groups, consumer groups, and other
case-oriented associations of clients, the public interest law
firm relied heavily on the reforming of judicial rules to facilitate the bringing of class actions and to provide for court-
ordered payment of attorneys' fees by losing defendants. Without such reform, the concerns of these groups might never
have reached the courts. According to Martin Shapiro, this
development enhanced democracy. "Now it was precisely their

lack of expertise that justified not judicial deference to administrators but judicial intervention. The heroic role of the judge becomes that of breaking into the closed circle of experts, subjecting their decisions to his and her own nonexpert surveillance as a lay representative of the lay public, and democratizing the technocracy by insisting on the access of all groups to the administrative process" (1982, p. 22).

In a small but highly significant number of cases, the courts began to enter actively into the management of public institutions, particularly schools, mental institutions, hospitals, and prisons. These interventions were normally prompted by the unsatisfactory conditions brought about by either a lack of state funding or standards, outright resistance of public officials to law change, or poor management practices of institutional officials (Horowitz, 1983). Moreover, intervention can be extensive. For example, Rosenbloom (1987) noted that in Boston in 1981 nearly half of the city's budget appropriations were presided over by federal and state judges.

More often, the courts stopped short of actually taking over the management of institutions, choosing instead to influence management practices indirectly. A good example of this type of judicial supervision was seen in *Griggs v. Duke Power* (1971), where the Supreme Court forced personnel policy (both public- and private-sector) to conform to the Court's own special interpretation of the merit principle in hiring practices. It established the principle that selection tools must be related to the job for which the application is made.

As a result of the Warren and early Burger Court rulings, agency decision making increasingly took on the trappings of the legal system. Hearing officers became more like judges in both their adjudicative and rulemaking functions, and lawyers' tactics and judicial rules of evidence more and more influenced the decisions made by these administrative tribunals. Further, all administrative decisions generated in administrative hearings came under greater scrutiny by the courts. State courts were as much involved in the policing and review of these practices as the federal courts because

most of the Supreme Court's rulings applied to state in-
strumentalities. These innovations went beyond the various
federal and state APAs to fashion new constitutional law mod-
eled on the need for broad and democratic representation,
easy access to decision makers, due process at the agency level,
and active judicial review of administrative action.

Nearly two decades after Earl Warren retired, the era of
the Court that bears his name still deeply influences the
nature of administrative justice at all levels of government.
Ironically, the influence of the Warren era may be felt more
in those states that have continued to have a liberal judiciary
than in the federal government, where a conservative judiciary
is rolling back some of the changes in that arena (Kincaid,
1988).

A Turn to Efficiency and Authority. Under the leadership of
Chief Justice Warren Burger, the Supreme Court began to
move away from a democratic, rights-oriented, and judicialized vision of administrative justice. In its stead, the Court
sought a model in which access would be carefully delimited
and administrative technical efficiency increased. In the
1970s, rising costs and mushrooming caseloads presented a
great challenge to federal courts and administrative agencies
alike. The Court was inclined to reduce both the types and
numbers of cases flowing through the agencies and thereby
reduce the workload of both the agencies and the courts.

According to Tribe (1978), a subtle shift occurred. The
Warren Court had favored relatively specific hearing procedures, both to protect an individual's well-established liberty
and property rights and to enhance the legitimacy of administrative adjudication through promoting participation. The
Burger Court approach was to design due process so as to
arrive at accurate decisions in a particular decision environment, one in which a citizen could demonstrate injury to a
well-defined legal right. The approach would balance promoting participation through the device of a hearing against
considerations of (1) the accuracy of administrative fact-finding in the absence of a hearing, (2) the costs involved in hold-

ing hearings, and (3) the significance of the matter in dispute (*Mathews v. Eldridge*, 1976, pp. 334-335). These considerations applied equally to the questions of whether any hearing should be held and, if there were to be one, the procedures required.

The Burger Court moved on several fronts to give greater latitude to administrators to devise decision procedures based on both expertise and efficiency. First, it reined in the expanding law of public official liability. First, in *Owen v. City of Independence* (1980), it opened the door for individual administrators, though not cities, to avoid liability upon a showing that action they had taken was in good faith and reasonable under the circumstances. Second, it encouraged the use of alternative dispute resolution techniques (ADR), including negotiation, mediation, and arbitration, to reduce the number of cases litigated. Third, in the *Vermont Yankee* case it began to back away from the use of judicialized procedure in rulemaking under Section 553 of the APA (Scalia, 1978).

Although the Burger Court retreated from the judicialization of agency rulemaking, it maintained or increased other aspects of judicialization. The pace of judicial interventions by both federal and state courts into the management of government institutions increased. Agency decision processes and decision settings continued to be heavily judicialized, and relief was selective and piecemeal. The Court continued to refine and clarify the new constitutional rights of citizens and public employees that had so occupied the attention of the Warren Court. But forces were now set in motion that would reduce judicialization. Participation, representation, guaranteed rights to hearings, and judicial review became less urgent. This was, above all, a period of consolidation and balancing after the explosive growth and change of the Warren era.

The Current Era. The year 1987 may have been a watershed in the history of the United States Supreme Court. The appointment of a new chief justice, William Rehnquist, working with a contingent of new associate justices—Sandra Day O'Connor (1981), Antonin Scalia (1986), and Anthony Kennedy (1988)—created the potential for major doctrinal change. Justice Scalia is a widely respected administrative law scholar with published and well-reasoned views. Like Rehnquist and O'Connor, he supported the exercise of agency discretion in a great majority of cases but is a strong supporter of subordinating administrative discretion to legislative intent where that intent is clear (Brisbin, 1990). In this constitutional fidelity to the majoritarian role of Congress, Scalia's vision is strongly reminiscent of that of former justice Felix Frankfurter.

What are the likely consequences of these directions for the quality of administrative justice? Combining the strongly positive response of the Court in general to permitting administrative and executive discretion with its preference for giving head to legislative intent, we may expect to find that it will be less tolerant of judicial and legal profession intervention into the affairs of the agencies, except where it believes the legislature has specifically willed that the Court retain an overseeing role. Further movement away from the Warren-era model of interest group representation is likely, at least in the federal bureaucracy. In the states, the picture is mixed. A substantial minority of state supreme courts, including those in most of the populous states, have maintained activist views of the role of the judiciary based on politically liberal interpretations of state constitutions (Kincaid, 1988).

The Rehnquist Court is not likely to maintain the protective view of both the Warren and Burger Courts toward the procedural rights of the poor and the underrepresented. In the federal judiciary and in the less liberal state judiciaries likely to follow the Supreme Court's lead, it seems likely that there will be a reduced willingness to review administrative action, a further restriction of administrative due process rights, and greater protections of public officials and perhaps state and local governments against personal liability, as well as changes in judicial rules of procedure, making participation in administrative forums more difficult. The prediction that the Rehnquist Court will move toward dejudicialization of the administrative process seems to be in line with an attitude of the professional bar that has been building for some time. According to Loren Smith, a recent chairman of the Administrative Conference of the United States: "To the extent that we judicialize government, we necessarily tend to see the failures of economic and social programs not as manifestations of wrong-headed policies, but as bad technique or the flawed work of wrong-headed administrators. Such an orientation paralyzes our political system, makes policy direction increasingly less relevant, and leads to increased dissatisfaction with government" (1985, p. 430).

The federal judicial establishment also seems to be inviting dejudicialization through innovation in dispute settlement methods by administrative agencies, particularly in the use of negotiation. For instance, agencies have been encouraged to experiment with alternative dispute resolution (ADR) techniques by the Administrative Conference of the United States and the American Bar Association (Lubbers, 1984). ADR methodology, which stresses negotiation, mediation, and arbitration, holds potential for increasing the efficiency of agency decision making, further decreasing the need for judicial review, and protecting the expectations and interests of affected stakeholders as participants in the policy process.

Lastly, pressure has been building in recent years to overhaul the federal APA. Scalia (1978) noted that the APA has remained unamended while vast changes have been occurring in the administrative environment, and it has become increasingly irrelevant due to special legislation that creates agency-specific procedures. Furthermore, the act has been weakened by the infirmities caused by original flaws and ambiguities that have gone uncorrected.

The Administrative Law Judge Debate. Administrative law judges (ALJs) are crucial components of administrative justice systems in the state as well as in the federal government. Federal ALJs outnumber federal trial court judges by two to one, process a larger caseload, and affect the rights of more citizens. They preside at formal administrative hearings in many of the federal agencies to resolve disputes involving the implementation by the agencies of public policy. In the federal government, the line or user agencies appoint them from lists prepared by the Office of Personnel Management, which examines the credentials and rates the applicants. Bar membership and activity as a judge, a trial lawyer, or an administrative law practitioner for a combined total of at least seven years is a necessary qualification. Federal ALJs hold their jobs permanently, based on good behavior. Their appointing agencies may take adverse actions against them after an opportunity for a hearing before the Merit Systems Protection Board (U.S. Office of Personnel Management, 1989). They are insulated by statute from agency investigative and prosecutorial personnel. Practices for hiring and employing ALJs and hearing examiners differ widely in the states.

Agencies are permitted to be more flexible than courts in their adjudication functions. Courts must generally keep their inquiries confined to the facts presented to them by the parties. However, "agencies are able to expand the formal record without the limits of strict rules of evidence or predetermined limits to the number of parties involved in the controversy. The aim is for the agency, through its quasi-judicial function, to decide a dispute as 'rightly' as possible with agency policy as the basic test" (Graham, 1985, pp. 260–261).

Over the years, ALJs have shifted increasingly away from rulemaking and an administrative perspective toward adjudication and a judicial perspective. Only 7 percent of federal ALJs presided at rulemaking hearings in 1982 (Graham, 1985). Graham concludes that the role of the ALJ is turning from its traditional emphasis on formulating agency policy toward simply "doing the right thing" when the agency is challenged. He worries, somewhat ironically, that the preoccupation with conducting formal hearings will leave ALJs short on effectively safeguarding the real (policy) rights of the parties appearing before them. As Chitwood concluded, "Only public administrators adequately trained in due process concerns and consciously sensitive to how their decisions

affect these fundamental rights [life, liberty, and property]
can offer the comprehensive protections constitutionally mandated for these interests" (1982, p. 43).

Increasing professionalism has been the rule in state
and federal hearing officer corps, which, predictably, has
brought ALJs and hearing officers into conflict with agency
administrators. The ALJs have become politically active in
representing and promoting their own interests. In the federal
government, executive branch pressures have come in the
form of demands to reduce case backlogs and increase accountability of ALJs for the "quality" of their decisions (often a
euphemism for the kind of decisions that the agency wants
in order to achieve economies). Federal ALJs have reacted
strongly to these pressures (Cofer, 1981; Skoler, 1982). Periodic
bills introduced in Congress call for a centralized organization
and autonomy for administrative law judges in a separate
ALJ corps. Several states have already created central hearing officer panels that separate the ALJs organizationally
(although not necessarily functionally) from their former agencies (Levinson, 1981; Rich, 1981).

A Critique of the Administrative Procedure Act. The administrative procedure acts, state and federal, have been much
criticized. In 1955, the second Hoover Commission admon-
ished agencies to engage in more rulemaking and to stop
making so much policy through adjudication (Cooper, 1988,
pp. 85–86). James Landis's report to president-elect Kennedy
in 1960 baldly asserted that the federal APA was a failure. He
found that administrative law problems had halted administrative planning and policy formulation; that lawyers were
practicing influence peddling; and that excessive delay, sloppy
implementation of procedural requirements, high costs, and
a basic lack of fundamental fairness were common problems
in formal administrative decision processes (U.S. Congress,
1960).

Other, "unofficial" critics of the federal APA noted a
fuzziness in the distinction the APA draws between a rule (the
product of rulemaking) and an order (the product of adjudi-

cation), with the consequence that an inappropriate forum is often used to resolve administrative justice issues (Davis, 1975, pp. 3–7; Scalia, 1978, p. 383; Bryner, 1987, p. 22). Scalia (1978, pp. 386–388) feared that the APA would grow increasingly irrelevant because Congress would continue in its habit of legislating procedural variations from the APA for specific agency settings, and the courts would use this confusion to make their own law.

Woll (1963) and Davis (1975) also cast doubt on the usefulness of APAs from the perspective of their inability to restrain most administrative decision making. Both documented that most significant dispute settlement involving administrative agencies is made through *informal* adjudication, which is not regulated by APAs. Agencies use informal process to gain program effectiveness and efficiency. They avoid formal procedure because it is time consuming, expensive, and geared more to lawyers' tactics and individual property interests than to accomplishment of statutory objectives, and because it invites judicial review (Woll, 1963, pp. 29–30). The implication is that APAs are simply inappropriate for most agency decision situations.

Despite this heavy load of criticism, the APA has persisted and found many supporters. Perhaps the most balanced and best reasoned view is that of Freedman, who, aware of the criticisms already noted, stated:

> But its strength, finally, lies in the fact that its provisions embody conceptions of elementary fairness quickly recognized as the basis of prevailing principles of procedural justice. The generality of the Act's major requirements has been a significant reason for its success in achieving a useful measure of procedural uniformity among agencies with very different regulatory responsibilities. It has been this generality of conception that has permitted judicial decisions applying the Act's provisions to one agency to temper and enrich decisions applying the same provisions to

other agencies. This achievement indicates why
the Act is properly regarded as one of the most
important developments in administrative law in
the twentieth century [1978, pp. 130-131].

Perhaps the greatest achievement of the federal APA has
been the service it has performed in helping to legitimate the
role of public administration in American government.
Despite the fact that most administrative disputes are handled
informally and thus are never touched by the APA, there is
utility to the proposition, and especially the perception, that
the agencies settle many of their most important disputes in a
climate of rational, unbiased inquiry guarded by standardized
procedural requirements and the watchful eye of a reviewing
court. Bryner puts it this way: "Most importantly, administrative law serves to legitimize administrative discretionary and
regulatory power. To paraphrase Thurmond Arnold's description of law in general, the function of administrative law 'is
not so much to guide society as to comfort it.' Administrative
law gives comfort and assuages the expectation that administrative power is constrained and checked" (1987, p. 31).

The point is well taken, and its logic may be extended.
Because the APAs are seen as structures and processes that
promote justice, they help to infuse public administration
with legitimacy. How much more legitimacy can be captured
by going beyond the statutory approach and creating within
administration a thoroughgoing concern for justice in all of
its decision processes?

Assessing the Effects of Administrative Law
as Administrative Justice

The legacy of the legal approach to administrative justice has
both positive and negative consequences. On the positive side,
administrative law doctrine and particularly the administrative due process movement has supplied public administration with many essential elements of justice. Due process
serves as the foundation for treating people fairly in dispute

settings, and it extends both procedural and many substantive rights that first emerged and were articulated during the Warren era. Administrative law generally has supplied incentives and the means to ensure that fair procedures are actually applied, not the least of which procedures is the potential for judicial review of administrative action.

On the negative side, the judicialization of more and more administrative decision making has reduced the effectiveness of administrative decisions. According to Freedman (1978, p. 47), this occurs in two ways. First, as agencies are required to follow judicial norms more closely, their capacity for effective decision making is weakened. Decisions become less politically relevant and less concerned with efficiency. Second, the legitimacy of administrative processes has suffered as agency expertise and commitment are called into question.

The lawyer's understanding of the world of administrative decisions, divided as it is into neat definitional compartments called "rulemaking," "adjudication," and "enforcement," and with its trust placed entirely in procedural safeguards to avoid administrative "abuse of discretion," is an artificial one at odds with the real world of politics and effective action. It is built on the notion that carefully conceived procedures will somehow secure justice. As we will see in the following chapters, seeking administrative justice in the true sense requires the decision maker to consider not only law and procedure but also public policy objectives, human behavior variables, philosophical principles, and organizational effectiveness. It is unreasonable to assume that any system of law, however well conceived and crafted, can deliver more than a portion of the forms, attitudes, skills, dynamics, and supports needed for the building of a sound administrative justice system. Many of the tasks of administrative justice require a different expertise than that which can be provided by lawyers and judges.

The social claim of the legal profession on the business of ensuring justice within public administration has been so powerful that academic public administration has almost abandoned the field. Practicing public administrators have become habituated to deferring to lawyers in much of the most crucial decision making that goes on in government.

It is ironic, yet probably understandable, that the voices raised most poignantly over the last generation in challenge to administrative legal orthodoxy are those of legal scholars. In the next chapter, we trace how these reflective thinkers have combined with persons from other academic disciplines and fields of practice—philosophy, sociology, psychology, labor-management relations, conflict resolution, and public administration—to give us a fuller vision of the relationship between justice, law, and administration.

3

A NEW PERSPECTIVE
ON ADMINISTRATIVE
JUSTICE

The administrative justice perspective developed in this book draws upon the contributions of scholars in a number of fields of study, including administrative law, behavioral theory, organizational theory, and public administration. Although the roots of these bodies of literature are fairly distinct, there has been considerable cross-fertilization in recent years. What has begun to emerge is a set of concepts and empirical findings that hold promise for integrating much of contemporary thinking about administrative justice.

In Chapter Two we described the view of justice in public administration that has prevailed in scholarly thinking and administrative practice in the United States over the last half century, a view that administrative law and the legal profession have defined and dominated. We described the shortcomings of this perspective, many of which the legal profession has described and debated. We also acknowledged the importance of the core elements of this traditional approach to administrative justice.

In Chapter Three, we briefly survey several other important contributions to our evolving thinking on administrative justice. We begin with the reform literature on administrative law, continue through the contributions of other fields of study and practice, and conclude with a summary of the key propositions that undergird the administrative justice perspective that we are articulating.

The Growth of New Administrative Law

The Conventional View. In Chapter Two, we presented an overview of the conventional view of administrative law, a view that has long dominated the legal profession's thinking about the relationship between law, justice, and the bureaucracy. It is characterized by the general belief that administrative justice can best be achieved through a formalized adjudicatory approach (the APA model), reinforced by judicial doctrines of administrative due process and the vigilance of the courts through their power of judicial review. Since the mid 1970s, however, an alternative conceptualization of administrative justice emerged among legal scholars. Sparked by the "due process explosion" and by the writings of Judge Henry Friendly, Jerry Mashaw, and others, a body of legal scholarship developed that takes exception to conventional legal thinking while adhering to its central tenets of fair process and judicial oversight. These advocates of what might be called the new administrative law challenge two core assumptions of traditional legal thought: the value of the adversarial process and the need for standardized formal procedures.

As we discussed in Chapter Two, conventional legal thinking held that it is necessary to tame the discretionary powers of bureaucrats because they are felt to be destructive of individual liberty and property rights (Dickinson, [1927] 1959). Justice inheres in the legal process, which is designed to benefit liberty and property rights. Bureaucrats are often seen as threatening these rights through "arbitrary and capricious" actions that deviate from the rule of law. The danger of such harmful action is best checked by trial-type procedures, by ensuring the use of lawyer advocates by affected interests in administrative settings, and by a judiciary that stands ready to review agency administrative action for conformity with the law and with judicially fashioned procedure (Jaffe, 1965).

The legal perspective on administrative justice was well put by John Dickinson ([1927] 1959), who wrote that administrative agencies paid less attention to procedural justice, lacked a coherent system of general rules, were preoccupied with drafting rules of general applicability, and were too close to politics. For Dickinson, administrative justice could best be achieved and legitimacy restored to public administration through regularizing administrative procedure, providing minimum procedural due process safeguards to those facing administrative adjudication, and making full judicial review available. The nation has taken precisely this direction, beginning with the enactment of the Administrative Procedure Act (APA) in 1946 and its progeny, the state APAs.

Horowitz (1977a) perhaps best summarized the limits of adjudication. Although he addressed the weaknesses of formal adjudication as a tool of policymaking in the hands of judges, he made his critique applicable to its use in administrative adjudication as well. According to Horowitz, formal adjudication has several weaknesses. First, judges are generalists and are incapable of handling specialized information in many fields. This criticism is equally applicable to administrative law judges (ALJs) and hearing examiners, especially when they are assigned to centralized panels. Second, the nature of formal adjudication is such that it is absorbed with the facts of a specific case, and it ignores facts in other cases that may be similar but are not before the tribunal. The result is that any policy lesson is limited and logically confined to the facts of the unique case. There is a danger, however, that the adjudicator and the agency may use the logic of the adjudication decision as a policy guide, applying it to other situations where it may not be applicable.

A third limitation of formal adjudication is that it focuses on issues of legal rights and therefore "inhibits the presentation of an array of alternatives and the explicit matching of benefits to costs" (Horowitz, 1977a, p. 34). Also, the adjudicator is passive with respect to issues that are to be adjudicated, reacting to the initiatives of specific parties in the context of a specific dispute rather than searching for facts relevant to solving broad-based problems. Adjudicative decisions are abstracted from a broader social context through a process that brings cases for decision that may not be representative. Moreover, the fact-finding process used in formal adjudication, conditioned as it is to judicial habits of applying rules of evidence, is ill adapted to finding the "social" facts that characterize the general nature of many administrative problems.

Finally, adjudication is "past-looking." Decisions are based on antecedent facts or behavior that predates the adjudication, so that adjudication is insufficiently attuned to what might happen in the future.

Of course, adjudication in the context of agency decision making has important advantages. It forces the decision maker to act, and to act with reference to evidence and reasoning. It may lend moral power to the decision by proceeding in a manner agreed to in advance and utilizing judicial rules of relevance not as subject to political influence. Further, ALJs and hearing officers themselves are less subject to political pressures than are agency personnel. In addition, it establishes a record of historical fact. It shifts decision responsibility to a neutral third party and thus tends to "depoliticize" controversy.

Nonetheless, the major argument by Friendly, Horowitz, and other critics remains valid: Formalized adjudication far too often is used inappropriately in situations in which informal adjudicative procedures, rulemaking, or negotiation would be more appropriate.

Administrative Law Reform. Beginning in the 1970s, reform-minded legal scholars have challenged conventional views of administrative law. Prominent among these "new administrative law" scholars are Judge Henry J. Friendly (1975), Paul R. Verkuil (1976, 1978), Kenneth C. Davis (1969), and Jerry L. Mashaw (1974, 1980). A major focus of their work has been the improvement of both the fairness and effectiveness of agency administrative decision making. The reformers accept in the main the APA approach, but they argue that means

can and should be found to improve agency administrative
hearing processes for the myriad adjudication and rulemaking
situations where APA-type procedures are inappropriate.

The administrative law reformers have several attributes in common: They accept prevailing legal norms regarding the antidemocratic tendencies of the administrative state;
they look for an optimum set of procedural elements, both
formal and informal, that will enhance the quality of justice
in the agency administrative hearing process; and they recognize that these elements will vary from situation to situation
and from agency to agency. They move beyond the lawyer's
customary image of adjudication as a decision process cen-
tered upon a trial-type evidentiary proceeding.

The reformers have drawn special support and inspira-
tion from the writing of the eminent federal jurist, Henry
Friendly. In a landmark 1975 essay titled "Some Kind of Hearing," Judge Friendly wrote about the "due process explosion," saying that "we have witnessed a greater expansion
of procedural due process in the last five years than in the
entire period since the ratification of the Constitution" (1975,
p. 1273). This led him to wonder "whether government can
do anything to a citizen without affording him 'some kind of
hearing' " (1975, p. 1275).

Commenting on the procedural protections mandated
by court rulings, Judge Friendly argued that the adversarial
process does not always serve the ends of justice in administrative hearings and indeed often is dysfunctional. He con-
tended that the most critical elements of adversarial procedure
should be reserved for matters of the most serious substance.
In descending order of priority, an agency action is of most
importance when it (1) deprives an individual of liberty, (2)
revokes a professional license, (3) terminates public benefits,
or (4) reduces public benefits (Friendly, 1975).

The most important of the procedural safeguards are
notice, opportunity for comments, and an impartial tribunal.
The less critical procedural elements include confrontation
and cross-examination of those giving negative evidence, a
transcript of the hearing, oral presentation, and the right to

call witnesses. These should not be allowed to burden hearings on matters of a lesser order of importance. In fact, they actually pose a danger of expanding the controversy (Verkuil, 1976). Again, agency administrative resources should be conserved and expensive trial-type procedures should be reserved for those hearings for which formal procedures are best suited and that involve the most serious substantive issues.

This notion of balancing hearing rights with other values, articulated in *Mathews v. Eldridge* in 1976, gave rise to a remarkably thoughtful and provocative critique of the existing administrative hearing system. Stimulated by Judge Friendly's work and the Mathews ruling, a group of administrative law reform scholars who came to be known as "mass justice theorists" sought to articulate a balancing or contingency approach. This approach weighs competing values such as accuracy, efficiency, and participant satisfaction in order to achieve a greater aggregate justice. The work of two of the mass justice theorists, Paul Verkuil and Jerry L. Mashaw, is especially relevant for our administrative justice perspective.

In his study of informal (non-APA) adjudication processes used in federal agencies, Verkuil (1976) identified three essential due process criteria: *procedural fairness, satisfaction* (participant trust in the process), and *efficiency* of the process (optimum resource allocation). Verkuil argued that, in general, the process should produce fair and accurate results, be seen as doing so by those involved in or affected by the process, and do so at the lowest system cost.

Balancing these three criteria requires employing the right mix of procedural protections for the specific decision context. Not all government decision making should employ the full range of procedures that are considered to provide due process protections. Providing trial-type procedures in inappropriate contexts not only would be costly to government but it also might not lead to greater fairness or participant satisfaction, especially where timeliness is a concern.

In agency adjudicative decision making, it is generally accepted that a measure of procedural protection can be fore-

gone in the interest of achieving greater efficiency under circumstances where (1) both parties have corresponding interests in a "correct" or "better" solution, (2) there are agreed-
upon standards for decision, and (3) there is a need for a
timely decision.

Verkuil found great variability in administrative practices in the federal agencies that he studied, but he also noted
that the agencies nonetheless provided a common threshold
of procedural safeguards. These included *provision of notice,
opportunity for written or oral comment,* and a *statement of
reasons* for the decision. What Verkuil found lacking was a
theory for refining the due process criteria and establishing a
methodology for applying the criteria to specific cases of informal adjudication (Verkuil, 1976).

Unfortunately, it is not possible to maximize all three
due process criteria in every informal adjudication situation.
In particular, there is likely to be tension between the value
of participation (which promotes trust in the process) and
that of efficiency (for example, in timely handling of cases).
To be effective, informal adjudication procedures must be
suited to each agency setting. The ability to develop an appropriate adjudication procedure lies with the agencies, not the
courts. The judiciary is institutionally incapable of effectively
assessing procedural requirements in agency settings. Fundamental reforms in agency procedures for informal adjudication can occur, but it is up to the agencies to lead the way
(Verkuil, 1976).

Mashaw's "dignitary theory" of administrative due process also challenges the notion that trial-type hearings are
always appropriate. His theory assumes the superiority of the
liberal democratic tradition of American constitutionalism
and focuses on "the degree to which decisional processes preserve and enhance human dignity and self-respect" (1981b,
p. 886).

Mashaw sees privacy constraints as fundamental to the
preservation of a political morality based on individual self-
respect. Individualization and direct participation present
"prima facie constitutional claims for realization" (Mashaw,

1981b, pp. 924–925). According to Mashaw, however, the consensus of liberal thought assigns a lesser importance to participation (1980, pp. 921–922). Rawls, for one, favors a system that is "reasonably designed to ascertain the truth" and views the administrative process as limited and instrumental to that end, not as a means to assure self-respect for those affected (Mashaw, 1981b, pp. 917–918).

What Mashaw ultimately seems to have in mind is what he calls a "relationship," a dialogue between the disputants that allows the parties to get to know each other and each other's interests. From this perspective, demands for participation take on life and energy. "Notions of equality and rationality that seem somehow sterile when they are interpreted as creating equal rights to pull a voting machine's lever and to receive a reason from an official are energized when they are reconceived as promoting an ongoing dialogue in a community of equals" (Mashaw, 1981b, p. 930).

Mashaw's dignitary theory represents a significant departure in thinking by administrative law scholars. He moves beyond the "new administrative law" scholars' concerns with reforming the existing administrative law system and heads toward the development of a broader theory of administrative justice.

Beyond Legal Reform. Mashaw's 1983 book, *Bureaucratic Justice,* is a major step toward the development of an integrated theory of administrative justice. In this study of the Social Security Administration's disability program, Mashaw went beyond a concern for balancing the process and organizational efficiency elements to recognize other relevant norms and values that bear upon making just decisions in bureaucracy. In doing so, he drew on elements of organization theory, economics, management science, and other disciplines.

Mashaw advances three goals of justice in benefits program decision making. First, decisions should be "accurate and concrete realizations of the legislative will"; second, they should provide "appropriate support or therapy from the perspective of relevant professional cultures"; and third, they should be "fairly arrived at when assessed in the light of traditional processes for determining individual entitlements" (Mashaw, 1983, p. 25). These goals lead to three models of administrative justice:

1. *Bureaucratic rationality.* Administrative justice is accurate decision making achieved through cost-effective processes. This is the classic bureaucratic model in which standard bureaucratic routines focus on making claims decisions correctly and efficiently.
2. *Professional treatment.* Administrative justice is having the appropriate professional judgment to one's situation in the context of a service relationship. This is a client-centered therapeutic model that recognizes the incompleteness of facts, the distinctiveness of the problems of clients, and the intuitive nature of judgment. Rules, hierarchical control, and efficiency are all subordinated to norms of the various professions delivering services.
3. *Moral judgment.* Administrative justice lies in the full and equal opportunity for individuals to obtain their entitlements. It is based on the traditional goal of the adjudicatory process to resolve disputes about rights, the allocation of benefits, and burdens. The end is a moral decision, a determination of who deserves what. The process is "value-defining" rather than implementing previously determined values, as in the bureaucratic rationality model.

Although Mashaw's models were developed as ideal types and reflect his extensive study of an agency specializing in large-scale benefits claims, they have broader utility. Examples of each type can be seen in many existing agencies, such as a public works department (bureaucratic rationality), hospitals (professional treatment), and regulatory agencies (moral judgment).

Mashaw contributes to our administrative justice perspective in two significant ways. First, his work is particularly important as a bridge between administrative law and our broader concept of administrative justice. It has helped to expand the boundaries of thinking about justice in administrative decision making in two ways: It has moved legal scholars' study of justice in bureaucracy beyond a narrow administrative law approach and it incorporates broader values in defining alternate justice models. The second contribution is that we have drawn on Mashaw's differing conceptions of justice in framing our own thinking, seeking to integrate them into a single multidimensional concept of administrative justice.

Behavioral Theory

Social scientists have become increasingly interested in the study of justice over the past twenty years, which results in some interesting theoretical developments and a growing body of useful empirical research (Cohen, 1986; Lind and Tyler, 1988). Scholarly attention initially focused primarily on distributive justice questions, but in recent years procedural justice studies have had an extraordinary growth. Although procedural and distributive justice are conceptually distinct, scholars consider them to be highly correlated. The interplay between them is not yet fully understood, however.

John Thibaut and Laurens Walker (1975) pioneered the empirical study of procedural justice. In the early 1970s, they conducted an extensive series of laboratory experiments using simulated court trials of disputes. Their resulting theory of procedure and the research it has spawned have important implications for practical issues in administrative adjudication. Thibaut and Walker's laboratory studies showed that the type of formal procedure used has an important effect on the satisfaction of participants and their perceptions of fairness. They reported that participants to a dispute prefer adversarial procedures that give them control of the process.

This conclusion brings Thibaut and Walker into conflict with the legal reformers, who argued that the adversarial system is not the fairest method under many of the circumstances that obtain in administrative systems. "[T]heir con-

clusions with respect to satisfaction and fairness would appear
to contradict those long held by procedural scholars from Ros-
coe Pound to Henry Friendly" (Verkuil, 1976, p. 754). Thibaut
and Walker (1978) later modified their position on the value
of adversarial procedures, arguing that procedures should be
adopted that are appropriate for the nature of the disputes to
be settled. For example, they suggest that the inquisitorial
(nonadversarial) model may be preferable under certain conditions, especially where the parties in the dispute have corresponding interests, where existing standards can be applied to
settle the dispute, and where time is a factor.

In the fifteen years since Thibaut and Walker's work
first appeared, the study of fairness in procedures has
expanded far beyond the formal trial settings of their ground-
breaking experiments. The settings for research on procedural
justice include citizen encounters with the police, court-
annexed arbitration, public school disciplinary practices,
parole revocation, performance appraisal practices, and the
grievance procedure (Lind and Tyler, 1988; Clark, Gallagher,
and Pavlak, 1990).

Research on the grievance procedure is especially significant because the grievance process is the carrier of due
process in the arena of employer-employee disputes. The grievance system is intended to prevent workplace injustice by
providing clear rules and regular channels of appeal, cul-
minating in a decision by an impartial outside arbitrator, if
necessary. Studies surveying labor union members show that
the grievance procedure is seen as a primary means for worker
"voice" in the workplace. Equally important is the finding
that the relationship between member perceptions of the grievance mechanism and union satisfaction is more closely tied
to member views of procedural fairness than to favorableness
of outcome (Sheppard, 1984; Clark, Gallagher, and Pavlak,
1990).

The developing body of empirical findings on procedural justice in many different settings suggests that, for procedures to be fair, they should provide opportunity for voice
and outcome control, be applied consistently, utilize accurate

information, provide for error correction, be representative, suppress bias, and be consistent with local ethics or norms. It should be noted that, with the slight alteration of a few words and the addition of the local norms consistency factor, this is the same list administrative law reformers developed.

Social psychologists have also studied the phenomenon of injustice, believing it to be a related but different phenomenon than justice. Using empirical methods, they have focused on a "sensitivity to injustice" in either the victim or in the victimizer and have studied the conditions that awaken and intensify this feeling (Deutsch, 1985, p. 50).

According to most of these investigators, the sensitivity to injustice among victims springs from feelings of relative deprivation in the distribution of benefits and burdens. If they feel relatively more deprived, even people who are well off in an absolute sense may be more discontented than those much worse off. Comparisons may be made between a single individual's actual condition and aspirations, or with another individual, or between a group that the individual relates to and some other group (Crosby, 1976). Moreover, people can distinguish feeling relatively deprived as individuals from feeling relatively deprived as members of a group (Runciman, 1966), and the former is worse. A person resents injustices that come suddenly and to one as an individual far more intensely than those one has learned to endure as a member of a group (for example, racial discrimination in employment), because they lack the emotional protection that comes from identification with the group (Crosby and Gonzalez-Intal, 1984; Greenberg, 1984). The size of the gap between what is received and what is believed to be due affects the magnitude or intensify of the sense of injustice.

Behavioral theorists' empirical research on justice issues in organizations has addressed issues of both distributive and procedural injustice. According to Deutsch (1985), a sense of distributive injustice can arise out of the circumstances accompanying any of the following: the nature of the good or harm being distributed, the identity or competence of those having a role in the distribution process, the styling and timing of the distributive decision, the values underlying the distribution (the "injustice of values"), the rules or criteria employed to represent the values (the "injustice of rules"), the way in which the rules are implemented (the "injustice of implementation"), and the way decisions are made about the foregoing (the "injustice of decision-making procedures").

Although sociopsychological research has proceeded in both distributive and procedural injustice, injustice associated with procedural phenomena has attracted the most attention in recent years. One exception was the work of Adams (1963, 1965), who found that the expectations that members of work groups hold with regard to the distributive shares they are due are affected greatly by a prevailing belief that the allocation of benefits and costs within a group should be proportional to the contributions of group members. He concluded that whenever workers were overpaid or underpaid relative to other workers who had made equal contributions, they would accordingly feel either guilty or angry. This body of research on procedural justice and the sense of injustice is important for our understanding of administrative justice primarily because it points to the importance to participants of fair decision-making procedures. It also begins to examine the linkage and relative importance of specific procedural elements to participant perceptions of fairness, sense of satisfaction with the process, and decision outcomes. Finally, it assists in examining the effectiveness and efficiency of different administrative process models in reaching correct decisions.

Conflict Resolution

Another stream of thought with great practical significance for administrative justice is found in the rapidly growing field of conflict resolution. Alternative dispute resolution (ADR), joint labor-management committees, employee assistance programs, ombudsman services, negotiated rulemaking, and other techniques have emerged as significant tools for managing conflict in a variety of organizational settings.

In some agencies, mediation, arbitration, and other third-party-assisted methods designed for surfacing and resolving conflict are employed as substitutes for long-established formalized adjudication and rulemaking. Two prime illustrations can be seen in the regulatory processes of the Occupational Safety and Health Administration (OSHA) and the Environmental Protection Agency (EPA). During the Carter administration, OSHA's posture was aggressive and confrontational, with much formal agency adjudication and court litigation resulting from industry appeals to safety code violations issued by the agency. Immediately upon the installation of more industry-sensitive administrators under the Reagan administration, OSHA adopted a much more conciliatory approach. The agency began to make extensive use of mediation techniques to work out educational programs to mitigate the causes of safety violations.

In 1983, EPA's Regulatory Negotiation Project began to use a technique called negotiated rulemaking to work out emission standards for woodstoves, underground injection control, and the removal of asbestos from school buildings (Fiorino, 1988). The objective of the negotiation is to reach a consensus that the EPA can then use as the basis for a Notice of Proposed Rulemaking. Working within the notice-and-comment format prescribed by the Administrative Procedure Act, the agency brings together representatives of affected interests to reach consensus on the content and possibly even the language of a proposed rule.

At first it may seem odd to see agencies only recently turning to alternative dispute resolution methods, because agency adjudication and rulemaking processes originally were thought to be responsive and flexible means for settling disputes. Many agencies were created precisely in order to meet a social need for the resolution of disputes that could not be resolved adequately in political or legal forums. Why should there be the need for alternative dispute resolution methods in government agencies? According to Philip Harter (1983–1984), pressures for using alternative methods arise because the increasingly judicialized nature of administrative processes has become a serious problem in many agencies. As administrative adjudication and rulemaking matured, judicial and legal profession practices and norms increasingly influenced them. As a result, they are less flexible and effective tools for resolving the disputes they were intended to resolve.

Deutsch (1973, pp. 72–73) highlights key features of an emerging new perspective on conflict:

1. Few conflicts are intrinsically and inevitably win-lose conflicts.
2. If the conflict is not by its nature a win-lose conflict, one should develop and maintain a cooperative problem-solving orientation that focuses on the interests of the different parties (and not their positions) and seeks a solution that is responsive to the legitimate interests of both sides.
3. A full, open, honest, and mutually respectful communication process should be encouraged so that the parties can clearly express and understand each other's interests with empathetic understanding; such a process will discourage the misunderstandings that lead to defensive commitments and to a win-lose orientation.
4. A creative development of a wide range of options for potentially solving the problem of the diverging interests of the conflicting parties should be fostered.
5. A sophisticated awareness should be developed of the norms, rules, procedures, and tactics as well as the external resources and facilities that are available to support good-faith negotiations and to deter dirty tricks, refusals to negotiate, and exploitativeness by any of the negotiators involved in a conflict.

Consensual approaches, whether traditional position-based negotiation or newer, interest-based negotiation, often provide fruitful alternatives to adjudication and rulemaking for public-sector dispute resolution. They are an increasingly important resource for public agencies, one which was not envisioned by traditional administrative law nor fully recognized by the legal reform school. The variety of consensual methods reflect such factors as voluntariness of participation, representation by counsel, third-party decision makers, formality of procedures, selection of law or some other criterion as the standard or basis for the decision, and the legal enforceability of the settlement (Ad Hoc Panel on Dispute Resolution and Public Policy, 1983, pp. 4–5).

Criteria used to judge the effectiveness of these dispute resolution procedures include the amount of delay, costs to the parties, extent to which disputes are resolved effectively at early stages, perceptions of freedom from retaliation, confidence in the procedure, and the effect resolutions have on the subsequent behavior of the parties (Kochan and Barocci, 1985).

Public Administration Theory Contribution

Our understanding of the nature and workings of justice in public administration has benefited greatly from the valuable contributions of a number of public administration theorists and public law scholars. The writings of Emmette Redford, Kennneth Culp Davis, and John Rohr are of particular importance for our developing concept of administrative justice.

Redford (1969) takes as his starting point four rudimentary principles of justice found in administrative law that have been used to protect citizens before administrative agencies: notice, the opportunity to be heard, a decision without bias, and independent review. As Redford says: "They cannot be implemented by law alone, and they do not meet all the needs for protection of the citizen. They cannot take the place of correction through political process, or of effective administrative organization and internal decisional processes. But they are essential for protection of the rights of men before administration and for embodiment of the democratic ideal in administrative practice. They are guides for nonlegal (informal) as well as legal (formal) administrative practice" (1969, p. 136).

He proceeds to develop the four legal requirements into administrative practice guidelines by noting the things that must be done to convert the bare legal protections into meaningful safeguards for citizens. The requirement of "notice" is converted into a democratic practice called "the right to know" by four means: (1) administrative arrangements for publicity of the legal protections and the affected rights, obligations, or entitlements; (2) private distribution of information to affected groups; (3) field contacts by administrators with citizens; and (4) independent study of the informal processes of administration and resultant publication of the findings.

The administrative equivalent of "the opportunity to be heard" is the right to access. Effectively granting access goes far beyond the mere "right to a hearing" granted by statute or court order and involves the following: (1) costs that may act as a bar to participation; (2) lack of effective group activity; (3) a proactive role for administrative agents in acting on behalf of individuals and unorganized interests, such as consumers; and (4) special administrative arrangements by which individual inquiries, petitions, and complaints can be pressed.

In administrative terms, a "decision without bias" means a fair forum. Beyond following the statutory provisions ensuring the independence of hearing examiners and screening from decision making those persons having a personal stake in the outcome, not much can be done to eliminate biases as to contending interests. This is because "administration is the servant of politics" and those who win the macropolitical process have built-in advantages "in the creation of official roles in administration that embody their interests" (Redford, 1969, p. 143). In addition, professional biases usually are present. Although bias cannot be eliminated, it can be mitigated by ensuring that all stakeholders are represented in any administrative policymaking meetings, and that the understandably biased allegiance of administrative personnel to policy objectives is tempered by a commitment to fair and humane consideration of individual interests in the context of particular cases.

Finally, the legal principle of "independent review" refers to the availability of judicial review. Redford argues that this falls short of what should be required on behalf of individuals subject to administrative power. Many persons cannot go to the courts because of the costs of court actions, the exclusion of some matters from judicial review, and the perceived inadequacy of available judicial remedies. The gap between judicial review and a real "right to appeal" may be met through a combination of devices, including appeals to legislators and an independent review within the administrative structure itself.

Administrative law scholar Kenneth Culp Davis has had enormous influence on public administration thinking about the proper use of discretionary authority. His classic book on administrative discretion, *Discretionary Justice,* is addressed to students of government and administration. In it, Davis argues that there is both too much unnecessary discretion and too little needed discretion in American government. He believes that "we should eliminate much unnecessary discretionary power and we should do much more than we have been doing to confine, to structure, and to check necessary discretionary power" (1969, pp. 3–4). The goal is to find the right mix of discretionary power for each administrative setting.

Davis acknowledges that injustice can occur when discretionary power is too limited as well as when it is too broad. When administrative discretion is too restricted, it is not possible to give adequate consideration to an individual's special circumstances or problem. Nonetheless, he argues that injustice is more likely to occur when discretionary power is too broad. He believes that this is a serious problem in American government, for 90 percent of administrative action is informal and involves discretionary power, is largely uncontrolled or unguided by established rules or principles, and, practically speaking, is not subject to judicial review. "The largest clusters of injustices in the entire legal system are in the area where these three elements come together," he maintains (1975, p. 158).

Davis believes that abuse of discretionary power is best controlled through the increased use of agency administrative rulemaking, not legislative enactments. He argues that administrators are best able to structure their own discretionary power because they know what specific administrative processes are involved in implementing public policies. Administrators need to be prodded, however, as they procrastinate in resorting to the rulemaking power to replace vagueness with clarity (Davis, 1969, pp. 56–59).

Our own view of administrative discretion is not nearly as mistrustful. While we share Davis's concern about the potential for abuse of discretionary authority, we are much less sanguine about the utility of administrative rulemaking. A far more promising avenue for structuring the use of administrative discretion lies in instilling in administrators and in the culture of their organizations a commitment to constitutionalism and associated values.

We experience this strong sense of constitutionalism in the writings of John Rohr. He makes a persuasive case for a normative theory of public administration that is based on the Constitution. "The role of the Public Administration is to fulfill the objective of the oath of office: to uphold the Constitution of the United States. This means that administrators should use their discretionary power in order to maintain the constitutional balance of powers in support of individual rights" (Rohr, 1986, p. 181).

Rohr sees public administration as a "balance wheel," in that it exercises all three powers of government and helps maintain an appropriate balance of power among the three branches. Public administration is subordinate to all three branches of government, making its contribution by "choosing which of its constitutional masters it will favor at a given time on a given issue in the continual struggle among the three branches" (Rohr, 1986, p. 182). To help it in making these difficult decisions, it should be guided by "constitutional principle." This combination of subordination and autonomy helps public administration fulfill its constitutional obligations while maintaining the autonomy necessary for professionalism.

Although Rohr does not explain which constitutional principle is to serve as the guide and how it is to be applied, he makes an important contribution to our concept of administrative justice by underlining the potential role of both multifunctionalism and subordination in the formation of a normative theory of public administration. "Multifunctionalism" refers to the lawmaking, law executing, and law dispute resolution activities of the three branches of government that are necessarily involved in the discretionary acts of public administration. All of these must be mastered in some way by public agencies. "Subordination" alludes to the role attitude that public administrators must assume, since they are not popularly elected. Although they must make law, execute law, and resolve disputes over law, they must do so in ways that the superior political branches would approve and find legitimate.

Rohr enriches our understanding of administrative justice by eloquently defending the constitutional legitimacy of public administration, by espousing constitutionalism as its normative base, by illuminating public administration's unique role as a constitutional "balance wheel," and by calling our attention to the importance of principled autonomy for the development of professionalism in public administration.

A Summary of the Key Propositions of Administrative Justice

We have thus come by a deliberate path to articulate a number of key propositions in an evolving model of administrative justice.

Chapter One argued that the primary concerns of administrative justice are (1) to bring about those outcomes envisioned by legitimately formulated public policies and (2) to treat people fairly in the process. The overarching principle is to serve the constitutions, laws, and regime values of

American political states. In doing so, the administrator sat-
isfies the basic requirement of justice, that of "giving each
person his or her due."

Chapter Two developed the theme that, regardless of
these overarching purposes of administrative justice, the field
of administrative law dominates the practice of administrative
justice and, through the partially inappropriate transplanta-
tion of legal values and excessive judicialization of decision
making in administrative agencies, has led it astray. Never-
theless, a basis was laid establishing a certain uniformity of
treatment in at least a range of disputes that imparted a degree
of consistency and legitimacy to the system.

In Chapter Three, we have examined some of the sem-
inal contemporary thinkers who either have thought about
justice in administrative settings or who have ideas about
justice that can be applied to administrative settings. It remains for us to distill this wealth of writing and thought to
discern its essential lessons.

The administrative law reformers' legacy is their pre-
science in knowing what must be provided before we can say
there is a fair process. They demonstrated wisdom in observing that a particular *and shifting* set of procedural elements is
necessary to achieve administrative justice in particular
agency settings and both formal and informal elements are
appropriate variables in the mix. These elements vary from
case to case, and from agency to agency, but include notice
and the opportunity to be heard, an impartial tribunal, participant satisfaction, efficiency (optimum resource allocation),
and the right to appeal.

Mashaw gave us insight into how different in nature
decisions can be, and how those differences can translate into
different justice needs. Some decisions are rational, analytical
analyses, calling for strict accuracy and application of the
legislative will. Here, adversarial hearings and participation
could be counterproductive. Other decisions are made in the
context of professional, therapeutic settings, as where a public
health professional must decide what course of treatment is
in the best interest of an individual or a family. Finally, there

are decisions that are of the nature usually assumed within the approach of the APA, those that are conflictual contests between contending interests. It is this last category that calls for the kinds of process element combinations considered by the legal reformers.

Redford's particular contribution is *seeing* that these *process* elements should be thought about in the administrative context. For instance, "notice" should be interpreted to mean that everyone likely to be affected by a pending administrative decision should be informed in a timely fashion that such decision is going to be made; in other words, they have the right to know what is being decided upon. Also, "opportunity to be heard" should be interpreted as a guarantee of the right to access, which means that affected groups and individuals be given the ability (financial help, assistance from agency experts, whatever it takes) to get their message accurately to agency decision makers. The "right to appeal," in the administrative context, means that persons who are adversely affected by initial agency decisions have the right to get an independent review within the agency as well as a clear path to external political bodies (legislatures and courts, primarily), in order to seek correction.

It is also a particular contribution of Redford to help us see that agency decision makers cannot be expected to be unbiased. Their constitutional oaths to execute the law and the fact of their employment in an agency understandably and properly bias them in favor of the administered policy. As a result, an inevitable tension arises between the justice that is due everyone under the policy and the justice that is due to individuals in the context of a particular application of the policy.

One type of bias that can and should be suppressed is the type that results in different decision outcomes in cases with similar or same-case scenarios. Davis (1969) is convincing when he argues that administrative agencies can do much to structure and check the use of administrative discretion to achieve consistency and equality of treatment. Redford would not disagree; in fact, the right to appeal he finds essential is

the type of structuring and checking that Davis has in mind
to prevent this kind of bias.

Social psychology, the conflict resolution literature, and
Mashaw all contribute to the understanding that a large part
of administrative justice relates to affective or psychological
variables. Social psychologists contributed the idea that the
sense of injustice has a psychological component that is only
partially addressed by the design of a fair process. Somehow,
it would therefore appear, provision must be made in the
totality of the agency's approach to administrative justice for
dealing with this psychological component. Whatever is done
will have to come to grips with what Mashaw means by
"dignitary theory," which involves the preservation and
enhancement of human dignity and self-respect. Through
their articulation of a variety of flexible techniques utilizing
third-party mechanisms of mediation, grievance procedures,
arbitration, and the like, writers on conflict probably have
taken strides to bring together concerns about the importance
of participation and self-control over outcomes, self-respect,
and cost and efficiency factors as well. The emphasis is upon
problem solving. Only in these ways can we hope to avoid
the effects of having "losers" emerge from the adversarial
contests that appeal so powerfully to the values of lawyers.

Finally, and very fundamental to the notion of true
administrative justice, is the matter of the administrators'
responsibility to seek just policies in the political realm, as well
as to correct, through the exercise of their own discretion, those
rules and operating procedures that stand in the way of implementation or fair treatment. This has two aspects. First, consistent with Rohr's principle of subordination, is the obligation
to pursue legitimate public policy. The second aspect is consistent with Davis's search for adequate administrative discretion
to do justice and Rohr's admonition that administrators should
use their discretionary power in order to maintain the constitutional balance of powers in support of individual rights. This
is the obligation of public administrators to go beyond a narrow, technical construct of their delegated duty and to be guided
by constitutional principle.

4

MAKING JUST
DECISIONS

It is generally acknowledged that decision making is a principal concern and central activity of public administration. As Harmon and Mayer express it, "Decisions are the core around which all other acts of the public administrator revolve" (1986, p. 5). Organizational decision making is commonly understood to be the process by which a course of action (or inaction) is chosen from among a set of alternatives in pursuit of organizational goals. What distinguishes public organization decision making is that the decisions are made in the name of the public and involve the use of public resources (Harmon and Mayer, 1986).

Decision making in public administration also is multifunctional, involving aspects of executive, legislative, and judicial functions. Decision making within these broad areas of administrative activity varies greatly in its scope and import, ranging from the routine, almost programmed application of a regulation or rule in an individual case to the formulation of wholly new policies and the design of new programs. Thus, the municipal housing department official reviewing a homeowner's application for a building permit to erect a garage on his property is engaged in administrative decision making. So is the state director of mental health mandated by the legislature to mount a coordinated government campaign to address an alarming rise in the reported incidence of teenage suicide across the state. Some administrative decisions—an informal interagency agreement on computer timesharing, for example—have relatively little direct impact on the daily lives of most citizens, while other decisions literally carry life-and-death consequences for large segments of the population.

Administrative decisions vary in other significant ways, including the monetary and nonmonetary costs involved, the degree of uncertainty that surrounds decision outcomes, the length of time for which the decision is to hold, and the moral or ethical implications of alternative courses of action. Similarly, the goodness of an administrative decision can be evaluated in terms of many different criteria, such as its timeliness, the degree to which it produces expected results, and its compatibility with existing organizational constraints. Administrative decisions also can be assessed in terms of the extent to which they meet standards of administrative justice.

Criteria for Just Administrative Decisions

Applying a justice standard to administrative decision making requires attention to both the outcomes of decisions and the processes followed in reaching them. Broadly speaking, administrative decisions are considered to be just to the extent that they (1) produce just outcomes (distributive justice) and (2) are produced by a process that is regarded as fair (procedural justice). There are several specific justice standards that are related to each of these categories.

Outcome Criteria. The outcome criteria for just administrative decisions follow logically from bureaucracy's role in the constitutional order. Because the bureaucracy occupies a subordinate position in our governmental system, broader questions of distributive justice are normally beyond the bureaucracy's scope of authority. Of course, most legislation requires that administrators "fill in the gaps," that is, make policy as part of their responsibility for implementing policy. For this reason, administrators inevitably make decisions that have distributive justice implications.

The purpose of administrative justice outcome standards is to help to ensure that "the people get their due." It is assumed that the legislature, court, or executive has acted in the public interest. The task of the administrator in carrying out the policy is to find and apply the operative principles contained in that policy.

The justice criteria that we discuss here do not serve to tell administrators which distributive justice standard (for example, need, merit, equality) to use in making specific decisions. In most public organization decision settings, distributive justice values do not have to be decided administratively. Rather, they are reflected in whole or in part in basic policy decisions previously made by legislative, judicial, or executive action. The political system has worked to produce the policy, and the administrator's responsibility is to implement it.

To guide the implementation of new legislation, for example, the lawmaker has made the language of the policy sufficiently clear, or guidance is available through legislative history, appropriation committee language, judicial dicta, attorney general opinions, or other information to illuminate legislative intent regarding the distributive standard sought by the law.

In the normal case, then, the issue is: How does public administration increase the likelihood that the type of distributive justice envisioned by the policymaker will be achieved? The administrator is constrained to follow a set of specific outcome criteria as a logical means to enforce the distributive justice standard dictated by the policy. To put the matter another way: Social justice requires that the administrator pursue the lawmaker's intent. For the bureaucrat to go beyond this delegated authority to create new and different distributions of social benefits and burdens would be an injustice and would lead to loss of legitimacy. As discussed in Chapter One, exceptions will exist for those occasions when the broader political-social policies or actions are so repugnant to accepted *general* notions of justice that, out of conscience, public administrators are compelled to reject them, as did the Danish bureaucracy in Nazi-occupied Denmark.

There are occasions when the distributive policy decision resides in the agency. First, for example, the legislature may have intended the agency to have a policy role and expressly granted it latitude. Second, the legislation may be ambiguous, either as the result of a political compromise in which it was necessary to leave some policy issues unresolved, or because of the inherent ambiguity of language. Third, the law's policy implications may not be fully understood, so that distributive policy issues arise in the course of implementing the law. Even when agency administrators have substantial discretionary authority, however, there will be a record of prior policy decisions, legislative debate, and other guides to the distributive justice objectives sought. Still, in these circumstances, the administrator must exercise judgment about which distributive justice standard(s) to apply.

Distributive Justice. Scholars have defined distributive justice in a number of different ways. Basically, it concerns the distributions that finally result from allocational processes. Distributive justice has been viewed variously as the treatment of people. All should receive outcomes proportional to their inputs, as equals, according to their needs, according to their ability, according to their efforts, and according to their accomplishments. They should have equal opportunity to compete without external favoritism or discrimination, according to the supply and demand of the market place, according to the requirements of the common good, according to the principle of reciprocity, and so that none falls below a specified minimum (Deutsch, 1975, p. 139).

In any given decision situation, these values may be in conflict. For example, treating people according to their ability may work hardship on those who are needy. Conversely, making decisions according to need may disadvantage those who have made the most effort. No one of these values can be claimed to have an inherent or natural priority; that is, which of the foregoing distributive justice values is to be given priority in a given area is always problematic.

For the public administrator, the overarching principle

is to serve lawful policy. In doing so, the administrator serves the basic justice principle of "giving each his or her due," as the political process in our constitutional system has determined. The following criteria may be applied to achieve just outcomes of administrative decisions:

1. The decision must be accurate or correct; that is, the substantive outcome of the decision process must fit the facts of the decision situation and the relevant policies and regulations must be applied appropriately to those facts.
2. The decision outcome must be rationally related to public policy objectives.
3. Decision outcomes must not violate the formal principle of justice: equal cases must be treated equally and, conversely, dissimilar cases must be treated differently.
4. Decision outcomes must reflect a balance between adherence to the rule and the exercise of discretion.
5. The decision outcome must primarily serve targeted client needs.
6. The decision must balance fairness to individuals against the social ends envisioned in the policy.

With each of these criteria, a primary concern is to serve the lawful public policy objective.

Accuracy. The decision may be considered just to the extent that it is accurate. Writing about the complex area of social welfare claims, Mashaw defines accuracy as "the correspondence of the substantive outcome of an adjudication with the true facts of a claimant's situation and with an appropriate application of relevant legal rules to those facts" (1974, p. 772). In a social welfare program, this means providing benefits to eligible individuals and denying the claims of those who are ineligible (1974, p. 779).

If we apply Mashaw's reasoning more generally to administrative decision making, accuracy can be viewed as the correspondence of the substantive outcome of the decision process to the facts of the decision situation, with an appropriate application of relevant policies and regulations to those facts. For example, if an agency's policy is to award merit increases and promotions based on job performance, a supervisor's performance appraisal of a group of subordinates is accurate if those who are recommended for merit increases are, in fact, the better performers. The decision by a purchasing manager to award a contract to the Acme Supply Company is accurate if, indeed, Acme is the lowest bidder who meets the specifications for the product or services to be provided.

As defined by Mashaw, then, accuracy is "the substantive ideal, approachable but never fully attainable" (1974, pp. 772-773). The value of an accurate decision will vary, depending upon the nature of the decision, the problem setting, and the cost of any change in the process calculated to improve accuracy. Thus, for example, accuracy is much more important in an administrative decision affecting the physical health and safety of a community than it is in a decision involving a simple appeal of a residential property assessment. The accuracy of the decision in the tax assessment appeal, in turn, has more importance than that required for issuing a small purchase order. That is, the cost of an inaccurate decision varies by decision case, as does the cost of obtaining the information needed to make a correct decision. The costs associated with high accuracy in decision making often may be too great, given the expected value of an accurate decision. A balancing is required, so that the process contributes to decision accuracy without being prohibitively costly.

Rational Relationship Test. A second output criterion is that decisions made by public administrators must stand in some rational relationship to public policy made by legitimate, democratically constituted political authority. They must be logically related to that policy and seek to further it. The rational relationship criterion is a necessary complement to the requirement that the bureaucracy be politically accountable.

It is important to make a distinction here between "policy as rule" and the "principle or purpose" underlying the policy. The policy principle, which is the desired outcome or the value that underlies the policy, is (or ought to be) superior to the policy rule (Dimock, 1980). The policy rule is merely a means for giving effect to the principle. If a policy rule does not serve its referent policy principle, the rule should be challenged and either modified or discarded, to satisfy the underlying demand of justice that the people for whom the policy was created receive their due.

In some circumstances, paradoxically, the administrator may be required to act contrary to rules or guidelines in order to achieve the law's basic purpose or intent. The administrator's challenge to an existing policy rule may be justified as providing either mid-course correction or needed feedback to policymakers so that originally intended policy objectives can be given effect (Burke, 1986).

The operative rules and guidelines may be in conflict with the policy principle for a variety of reasons. First, the policy may be poorly designed. Policymakers, including perhaps the agency leadership, may have chosen inappropriate means for arriving at desired outcomes. Second, the conflict may reflect basic disagreement between branches of the government, as when the executive branch seeks to evade the intent of a law by adopting regulations that thwart the policy purpose. Executive branch officials may have philosophical or political differences with the lawmakers, or successful implementation of the law may threaten their personal interests.

The faulty design of the means to reach policy ends is a common occurrence and frequently is rational from a political standpoint. A poorly designed law may be the result of a political compromise necessary to get the law passed or to obtain policy approval in the first place. The desire to get some kind of law passed leads to agreement to include provisions that *intentionally* weaken or undermine the policy's effectiveness.

A good example of injustice arising from the failure or inability of an administrative agency to apply the rational relationship criterion can be seen in the implementation of the Occupational Safety and Health Act of 1970. The act required the Occupational Safety and Health Administration (OSHA) to adopt regulations incorporating industry standards of safety soon after the act's passage. It also gave little discretion to OSHA inspectors, requiring them to issue a citation for every violation, even if the employer corrected the violation on the spot (Bardach and Kagan, 1982). Inspector performance was evaluated in part based on the number of violations cited.

The result was that OSHA was put in the position of having to enforce a set of inflexible rules that often worked irrational hardships upon the regulated (Bardach and Kagan, 1982). The highly laudable statutory principle—the improvement of worker safety in the workplace—was undermined by a rigid, poorly conceived statutory plan of implementation that also hurt the reputation of the agency charged with its enforcement. The responsibility of agency administrators in such untenable circumstances is to provide feedback to the legislature on the ineffectiveness and unintended consequences of the mandated policy rules, while using whatever discretionary authority is available to them to mitigate the harmful consequences of the rules.

The Formal Principle of Justice. A third criterion is that decision outcomes must observe the formal principle of justice: like cases or individuals should be treated alike and, conversely, dissimilar cases or individuals should be treated differently in proportion to their dissimilarity. This principle is a necessary condition for the existence of distributive justice (Frankena, 1975). Justice does not necessitate treating everyone in an identical manner. Indeed, as Aristotle argued, treating unequals in the same manner is as unjust as treating equals unequally.

Yet it does not follow that all cases in a class must be treated alike according to a general set of rules. Rules are imperfect and their strict application can be expected to result in an injustice in some number of cases. Therefore, there is need for continuing refinement of rules so as to limit the number of unjust results (Wasserstrom, 1975).

Consider the case of two property owners who fail to pay the real estate taxes they owe to their municipal government. Both are liable, yet there is a significant difference between the elderly, impoverished widow who cannot afford to pay her overdue tax bill and the unscrupulous slumlord who ignores tax notices as she schemes to squeeze profits from a piece of rental property. To treat each case the same would scarcely be thought just. As Carl Pinkele so ably put it, "Justice blind to the human facts of a case runs a very great risk of being blind justice" (1980, p. 11). Justice often can be achieved through a close examination of the specific facts shaping the background of each case, something Brian Barry (1965) calls "background fairness."

The Food and Drug Administration (FDA) policy for approval of new drugs requires a lengthy period (about seven years) of scientific experimentation. About 20 percent of the applications for the new drugs eventually are approved. The purpose of the FDA drug-testing policy is to assure the safety of and public confidence in *all* new drugs. Groups representing AIDS sufferers have pressed for acceleration of the testing period and permission to use drugs that are believed (often on scant evidence) to be effective in treating AIDS or its effects. The FDA cut the approval period to eighteen months for the drug AZT, a period faster than for any drug in FDA history. Is the special treatment of AIDS-related drugs by the FDA a violation of the formal justice principle? Does the urgency attached to treating persons who would probably die more quickly without the drug warrant this exception to FDA policy? It presumes that AIDS patients are in an essentially different position from patients suffering from terminal forms of cancer or other fatal diseases. Further, it fails to consider that in rushing AZT to market the general public may be put at risk or may not fully benefit from the drug.

Conflicts inevitably will arise in the application of formal justice to concrete situations. Particularistic treatment of a unique case may provoke charges of "favoritism" by claimants whose cases are regarded as being more routine and, therefore, requiring less attention. Conversely, bureaucracy's desire for universality and neutrality in decision making risks having unique cases "fall in the cracks" of a system of rules and standardized procedures.

The formal principle of justice necessarily requires public administrators to implement policy consistently. An injustice may occur when the decision deviates from the correct or uniform application of the policy or rule, with the effect that like cases are not treated alike. The root cause of this type of injustice may be a poorly defined policy or rule, or it may be the inconsistent behavior of the individual decision maker, or it may be inconsistent behavior across a range of decision makers.

Individual decision makers act inconsistently for a variety of reasons. For example, they may have taken inadequate notice of the policies or rules in effect. Or they may be acting for personal reasons or motives, ranging from self-interest to bias. They may be under pressure from their organization to serve an agency interest that conflicts with the policy or rule. They may have changed their interpretations of the meaning of the policy or rule and how it should be applied. Each decision maker undoubtedly brings to bear on a decision a unique background and personality, virtually assuring that there will be differences in how and what each decides.

A unique case in which inequality in the treatment of similarly situated persons may be defended is in research settings where the study design calls for a benefit (or risk) to be given to an experimental group and withheld from a control group. This procedure is defended on the grounds that the experimental research design leads to greater scientific validity of findings than other methods and, therefore, to better informed public policy decisions. It is argued that fairness requires only that the subjects of the research knowingly consent to the procedure and that members of treatment and control groups be assigned randomly. It is nonetheless true that administrative decisions are made that impart an unequal benefit or risk to cases similarly situated. The question becomes: Does the enhanced learning that comes from employing the experimental research model justify violation of the formal justice principle? Is the deviation from the formal justice standard warranted in terms of the larger benefit to society (including those who may be disadvantaged by the experiment)?

What about the pilot program in which one community is singled out for special treatment and the effects are compared to outcomes in control group communities that are denied the treatment or benefit? Political or other motives not having to do with knowledge advancement may be pointed to as the reason for the choice of the community to be favored. Under such circumstances, random methods for the choice of the experimental group is necessary to the preservation of equal treatment as well as scientific rigor. Further, it is desirable to extend the policy experiment so that the control group communities could enjoy the treatment or benefit while not compromising the policy evaluation. In some policy experiments, for example, the control group community in the first cycle of the program becomes the experimental group for the second round, with a third community assuming the role of control group for that round, and so on through the life of the project.

Balancing Rule and Discretion. A fourth output criterion, and one that is closely related to the formal justice principle, is that administrative decision makers must strike a balance between adhering to formal rules and exercising administrative discretion. It is almost universally recognized that discretionary authority is necessary for effective public administration (for example, Waldo, 1948; Davis, 1969; Rohr, 1978; Cooper, 1983).

Often the administrator's discretionary authority is granted specifically by law, as when a statute declares that "the Secretary may, in his discretion . . ." More often it is couched in a less direct, albeit clear statutory provision conferring discretionary authority.

Lack of meaningful discretionary authority is likely to produce unjust decisions, particularly when administrators must apply general rules in concrete cases. For example, Bardach and Kagan (1982) convincingly develop the case that the law's insistence that OSHA inspectors enforce rigid and often ill-fitting industry guidelines against plant and factory owners led to absurd, unjust results and reduced respect for the regulators. Excessive constraints on bureaucratic discretionary authority often lead to the bizarre cases reported in the media, such as the recent incident in suburban Richmond, Virginia, where an eight-year-old girl was suspended from school and reported to the Henrico County police for illegal possession of an alcoholic beverage. Young Haley Woodfin also was referred to juvenile intake proceedings, where she reportedly must undergo counseling. What offense had little Haley committed to warrant such seemingly strict treatment? She brought to her third grade "show and tell" an unopened can of "Billy Beer," a collector's item, from a display case at home. Although the initial school system decision to suspend Haley and to report her to the county police can best be characterized as poor use of discretionary judgment, the police department's action in referring the young girl to juvenile intake reflects a perceived lack of discretionary authority, given a strict departmental policy on the handling of complaints of illegal possession of an alcoholic beverage by a minor.

As these examples amply illustrate, discretionary authority is vital for tailoring decisions to meet the unique properties of different situations. Conversely, too broad a discretionary authority may lead to violations of the formal principle of justice through the dissimilar treatment of cases that are essentially similar in their factual bases. This problem is readily seen in the criminal justice area of parole supervision. Parole officers from neighboring districts, or even within the same district office, may impose widely diverging punishments for parolees who have committed the same types of parole violations and have similar background characteristics. One parolee who fails to keep a scheduled meeting with his "PO" may get a warning while another, less lucky parolee is "violated" by a tougher colleague.

The core problem is one of finding the proper balance between the need for uniformity of treatment and the need for official discretion to permit special tailoring for unique and unforeseen circumstances (Bardach and Kagan, 1982). Unjust decisions are more likely when the balance is tipped in either direction. Davis (1969) couples the recognition of the necessity for discretionary power with the prescription that administrative agencies must themselves structure, confine, and check their exercise of discretion, rather than looking to the courts or legislatures to do these tasks for them. This prescription finds spirited opposition among some legal scholars, such as Judge J. Skelly Wright (1972), who believe that administrators are not to be trusted and see no option but for the courts to play a continuing and vigilant "watchdog" role.

The need for balancing administrative discretion and rules also finds support in the writing on "street-level bureaucracy." Lipsky defines "street-level bureaucrats" as those public service workers who have direct contact with client groups and the public and who have substantial discretionary authority (Lipsky, 1980). The prototypical street-level bureaucrats are our cities' public school teachers, police officers, welfare workers, and other front-line providers of service, often to nonvoluntary clients. Because they have to cope with difficult situations, inadequate resources, and conflicting demands and expectations, street-level bureaucrats require considerable discretion and freedom of action in order to be effective in carrying out their responsibilities. The danger of a broad grant of discretionary authority is its potential for abuse.

Serving Client Needs. The fifth criterion is that the decision outcome should not serve the organization's or individual administrator's interests at the expense of targeted client and service needs. Organizational decisions tend to drift over time toward serving means and "displacing goals" (Merton, 1949) or maintaining the influence of a core group of organizational members (Michels, 1962). Bureaucracies also have the tendency to develop ongoing working relationships with key legislative committees, stakeholder groups, and other potential bases of support. The agency may then find it difficult to keep a clear sense of exactly who its clients are.

Thus, one criterion by which to judge the justice of decision outcomes is the extent to which the organization's decisions place the interests of those whom it is intended to serve above its own interests. Similarly, administrators' decisions should not be based on their personal interests or simply reflect their personal, moral, or political predilections. Public administrators are, or have the opportunity to be, in close interaction with citizens at the receiving end of government services and regulations. The standard of serving client needs requires administrators to be attuned to the needs and unique circumstances involved in their transactions with citizens (Harmon, 1981).

Balancing Individual Fairness and Social Purpose. A final criterion is that the decision must strike a balance between individual justice and social justice. Donald Horowitz (1977a) uses these terms to define and describe the tension existing between traditional legal thought, which emphasizes the use of process to ensure a fair outcome for the parties in a particular case, and traditional organization theory, which emphasizes rational inquiry that promotes policy goal attainment. Thus, administrators must strive to reach decision outcomes that are fair to the parties directly involved but do not sacrifice the larger public policy purpose that serves the many.

The recent controversy over the Food and Drug Administration's handling of the experimental drug AZT is a prime example of the decision dilemma: Should the FDA rush the drug to approval so that it may benefit thousands of victims of AIDS, or should it follow its standard policy of careful, cautious testing to ensure that the drug is properly certified and its risks and benefits are more clearly known?

The balance problem is one that continually faces large-scale benefits or case management programs, where the cost of handling an individual case must be balanced against the need to respond to many others. For example, consider the appeals process for Social Security Administration (SSA) disability benefits. A person whose initial claim for disability benefits is denied has the opportunity to appeal through several levels of the SSA appeals system, which is designed to ensure accuracy and fair treatment in SSA claims adjudication. As structured, the cost to the individual of appealing a negative decision is relatively low, while a positive decision at any stage of the appeals process signals a successful claim. The process is costly to the agency, however, and diverts resources from other positive uses. At what point does the agency decide that providing procedural safeguards to ensure making an accurate decision on an individual claim is too costly, given the agency's responsibilities to other claimants?

Process Criteria: Procedural Justice

In addition to assessment of decision outcomes by justice criteria, administrative systems may be judged by the fairness of the processes that produce the decisions. Decision processes are important in our political culture, which places value on fair procedures for their own sake: *How* decisions are made often is considered more important than *what* is decided. Procedures are important because they serve both instrumental and value-expressive purposes for people (Tyler, 1986). By "instrumental," Tyler means that in general fair procedures are believed to generate fairer outcomes than do unfair procedures. By "value-expressive," he means that some elements of procedure are valued for their own sake; for example, they provide for participation or "voice" and the opportunity to "tell one's side of the story."

Decisions are thus more likely to be accepted as legitimate when the decision process is regarded as fair. Paradoxically, the concern for fairness in procedures also may lead to complaints by some of bureaucratic "red tape," forgetting that "one person's 'red tape' may be another's treasured procedural safeguard" (Kaufman, 1977, p. 4). Core criteria for assessing the fairness of decision processes include equality of access, neutrality, transparency, efficiency, participation and humaneness, and the right to appeal.

Equality of Access. First, the decision process may be considered just or fair to the extent that there is equality of access to the decision maker by those whose interests are affected by the administrative action. This includes access (directly or indirectly) to decision forums, access to information, ability to open issues for public discussion, ability to assert one's claims without fear of coercive retaliation, and the right to consideration of all claims that are asserted (Redford, 1969). Of particular concern here is the unfair advantage that may be held by stakeholder groups having greater material and organizational resources, a particular problem with adversarial decision processes, as they tend to reward legal, investigatory, lobbying, and presentational skills that must be purchased.

Neutrality. Second, decision processes generally are considered to be fair to the extent that decision makers are neutral and impartial. According to Kenneth Culp Davis, four types of bias can be found in the deliberations and decisions of neutrals.

The first type of bias occurs when the decision maker has a preconceived point of view about issues of *law or policy.* In this sense, most of us have a bias—for liberty or property interests, in favor of limited government, or for a social welfare state, for example. It is impossible to think about any issues of significance without forming an opinion. What is difficult is to identify the dividing line between a proper attitude on a policy issue and an "excessive zeal that should disqualify" an administrator from making a decision or taking action because of improper bias (Davis, 1975, p. 176). The problem of bias relates to the administrator acting in the role of neutral. A policy bias may lead an administrator to prejudge a decision problem in a particular case, to the neglect of developing relevant decision alternatives and seeking necessary information for informed decision making. When this occurs, the decision process cannot be said to be fair.

The second form of bias relates to a prejudgment concerning issues of *fact* about the parties in the issue to be decided. This is also problematic, as too great a bias of this type can lead to an unfair decision. Suppose, for example, that a question arises over the establishment of a field office for a county program serving the elderly. The administrator who will decide the issue calls a staff meeting to hear the differing viewpoints. As the meeting unfolds, the administrator increasingly screens out the arguments in favor of creating the new field office. He has already decided against it, based on some population data that he saw some time ago suggesting that there are too few elderly persons living in that area who would be eligible for the program's services.

The third form of bias is what Davis calls "partiality" or "personal bias" or "personal prejudice," which indicates a disposition in favor of or against a *party*. Consider the case of an informal meeting to discuss employee Smith's complaint that his section supervisor is "dumping all the little dirty jobs" that need to get done in the office. If the superior who is acting as a neutral has made a prejudgment that the employee is a malingerer and is dishonest, the danger is that Smith will not get a fair hearing. The balance is difficult to assess here, as decision makers often bring to a decision prior knowledge that can be either very valuable or prejudicial.

Another form of personal bias occurs when administrators impose their own expectations and interpretations of reality upon the clients with whom they deal. This is particularly likely to occur when the poor encounter bureaucracies, for bureaucratic organizations tend to reinforce the class structures of the community (Sjoberg, Brymer, and Farris, 1966). This clash of values between a predominantly middle-class bureaucracy and the lower-class client holds considerable potential for bias in treatment by administrators.

The fourth type of bias is *"interest."* This can occur where the decision maker stands to gain or lose by a decision either way, such as when a member of a zoning board votes for a variance that would benefit his own property, or when a hospital administrator asks to place a relative on the payroll.

Practically speaking, the degree of impartiality or neutrality required will vary according to the importance of the decision and the cost of ensuring that bias is absent. Thus, it may be acceptable for a supervisor to conduct a performance appraisal of an employee with whom he has had a personal dispute, provided that there are available appeal mechanisms should the employee feel that the appraisal is unfair. Conversely, it may be impossible to justify an administrator's authority to award a contract in a case in which a firm in which he has a significant financial interest is a bidder.

Transparency. A third justice criterion by which to judge a decision process is what Mashaw (1983) calls its transparency, that is, its *openness* and *comprehensibility*. Mashaw means that those whose interests will be affected by the decision must have adequate notice of the issues to be decided, the evidence or information relevant to those issues, and how the process itself works. Finally, there must be some assurance that the expressed issues, evidence, and process are in fact meaningful to the decision outcome, an assurance generally provided by the administrator's explanation of the basis for the decision. Transparency of the decision process enables those who are affected by administrative decisions to participate meaningfully in the process and also contributes to their sense of dignity.

Because of the technical and procedural complexity of many administrative decisions, transparency may be difficult or costly to achieve. Consider the problem in many benefits programs in urban areas serving large numbers of non–English-speaking persons. How can the agency provide adequate notice of the benefits and rights available to eligible persons? Should it provide native language program materials for each of tens of language groups? These are just a few of the thorny questions relating to decision process transparency that face administrators who manage programs serving new immigrant groups.

Another interesting and complex issue of openness concerns the amount of information a benefits program agency should supply to claimants. Should the Social Security Administration, for example, inform disability insurance program claimants only of their rights to appeal a denied claim, or should it also tell them of their relative chances for success? By not providing this additional information, the agency may be discouraging frivolous or fraudulent appeals, but it also may be denying benefits to many deserving claimants who do not appeal because they think their chances are slim. These claimants might well change their minds if they are informed that their chances of a successful appeal are, say, 50 percent. In fact, Mashaw reports that the success rate of appeals in fiscal year 1979 was over 70 percent (1983, p. 42).

For many types of administrative decisions, the ability to have competent legal, financial, or other professional counsel may be crucial to citizens and government employees for understanding the form and the workings of the decision process. Transparency then becomes transformed into a question of wealth, organizational resources, and access to information needed for meaningful participation in the process.

Efficiency. A fourth process criterion is administrative efficiency, especially salient when the responsiveness or timeliness of the decision is an important concern. "Justice delayed is justice denied" is an apt description of the costs of decision delay in many instances. The most thorough, meticulous decision process is of little value if it fails to produce timely decisions.

Consider the problem facing persons who have filed complaints of discrimination with the New York State Division of Human Rights. The agency mediates complaints of discrimination in employment and housing, serving those who cannot afford the expense of going to court with a civil suit. It provides free legal help and, after hearings before an administrative judge, can compel payments, job promotions, or housing arrangements to redress bias. But because of increased workload and budget cuts, the agency is swamped with work. A backlog of more than 11,000 cases awaiting a "first investigative outcome" is forcing some people to wait as long as seven years for a resolution of their complaint. Of those cases, more than 4,000 were more than two years old and about 10,000 were more than six months old. It takes so long to settle cases that the final judgments can be rendered almost meaningless (Verhovek, 1989).

The importance of timeliness varies by decision setting, but clearly there are often trade-offs between decision timeliness and other process values, notably accuracy, participation, and cost. The increase in accuracy gained by spending more time and staff resources on a decision problem may be counterproductive if the value of the decision rests (at least in part) on its timeliness.

Administrative efficiency also can be viewed from a straight cost-effectiveness perspective: The more efficient the decision process is, the greater the number of clients that can be served and/or the greater the amount of scarce public resources that can be directed to achieve policy goals. In this sense, administrative efficiency can serve both procedural and distributive justice. When efficiency is seen as the dominant organizational value, however, the likelihood of administrative injustice increases as other justice criteria are disregarded.

For example, holding public hearings on proposed changes in state regulations governing the mainstreaming of children with handicaps into the regular school systems' programs is less efficient than simply announcing the changes. But the hearings fulfill an important agency responsibility for public participation and accountability. The problem lies not in the norm of efficiency per se but in a concern for efficiency to the exclusion of other important values.

For example, David Burnham (1989) reports in his recent book on the Internal Revenue Service that, in their zeal to feed the treasury, IRS agents all too often overstep their authority. Burnham cites IRS activities ranging from planting illegal wiretaps to imposing extra charges in order to meet agency production quotas. This is not unlike the speeding ticket quotas police officers in some departments are required to fill, the existence of which the departments vigorously deny.

There is a direct and positive relationship between efficiency and the substantive criterion of accuracy. Evidence must be assembled in relatively complete fashion and be available at the time agency decision makers decide upon claims. An outstanding example of the relationship is given in the June 1988 announcement by the Veterans Administration that they had discovered ten million military medical records, some of which duplicated records lost in a 1973 fire. Many claims of World War II and Korean War veterans were rejected earlier for lack of evidence that could have been available if either the records had been better secured against fire or the duplicate files had been discovered earlier (Putnam, 1988). More efficient practices that would allow VA officials to know about and have access to duplicate files would greatly further the cause of justice.

Participation and Humaneness. A fifth process criterion is participation in the decision process by those whose interests are affected. Participation serves not only the immediate need to protect the interests of those directly affected by the decision but also the enhancement of individuals' sense of being treated fairly (Thibaut and Walker, 1978). What is not fully clear is the type of decision process that best supports perceptions of meaningful participation and, therefore, feelings of self-respect and dignity.

To be meaningful, participation must include at a minimum (1) access to information, (2) access, either direct or indirect, to the decision forum, (3) the ability to raise issues for discussion, (4) the ability to assert one's claims without fear of coercive retaliation, and (5) consideration of all claims asserted (Redford, 1969, p. 8). A corollary participation value is the humaneness of the decision process, that is, the degree to which it promotes the humane treatment of the participants. As Mashaw (1983) notes, the problem lies in determining what is humane treatment in any given decision setting, for people may have differing preferences concerning how they should be treated.

The Right to Appeal. The last criterion discussed here is the availability of an appeal from an administrative decision. The purpose of this device is the prevention of wrong decisions or decisions that are not sufficiently comprehensive. This feature is associated with hierarchy and is regarded by Emmette Redford (1969) and Paul Appleby (1969) as basic to democracy.

The likelihood of an appeals process producing an inaccurate or unfair decision increases when the prescribed avenues of appeal are overcrowded, when they are difficult to use, or when the administrative agency actively discourages their use. Although it may be just in every other particular, a decision process that lacks an effective means for correcting decision errors can be fatally defective. Does this mean that a wrong decision is, ipso facto, unjust? We do not think so. However, an administrative system that does not acknowledge the inevitability of wrong decisions by making provision for their correction is an unjust system.

An example of an appeals process that generates inaccurate decisions is the general pattern of property assessment appeal and review procedures used in most local governments throughout the United States. These systems are frequently characterized by unannounced and poorly explained fractional assessment practices by assessors, lack of timely notice of assessments and explanation to taxpayers as to how they were derived, withholding of information on the valuation of similarly situated property, a limited period for the filing of appeals, and overreliance upon the word of the assessor by politically constituted appeal boards (Pops, 1985).

A Summary of Criteria for Making Just Decisions

Applying these administrative justice criteria in actual decision situations is not an easy task. The decision problems often are characterized by moral ambiguity, complexity, and indeterminacy; in any given decision situation, some of these justice principles are likely to be in conflict. When this occurs, difficult choices have to be made from among principles which, although compelling when considered separately, cannot be satisfied simultaneously. There are no simple decision formulas available to administrators for resolving these value conflicts. Still, the absence of unambiguous guidelines does not relieve public administrators of the responsibility to act justly.

The identification of criteria for making just administrative decisions is but the first step in the construction of a framework for a just public administration. The next steps in the process move us from the level of analysis of a just decision to the context in which it is made, the public organization environment. It avails us little if we know what criteria to use in making just decisions but we cannot apply them meaningfully because of the existing structure, climate, behaviors, management practices, or technologies in our organizations.

The organization setting for administrative decision making is therefore the subject of the next chapter, followed by an exploration in Chapter Six of the role and responsibility of the individual administrator, the common denominator between the making of a just decision and the building of just organizations.

We judge administrative actions taken in implementing public policies by asking whether the action is rationally related to lawful public policy objectives, is accurate, follows the formal (equality) principle of justice, reflects a balance between rule and discretion, serves targeted client needs, and balances the need for fairness to individuals with social or aggregate justice. We judge administrative processes to be fair when they provide equality of access, openness and comprehensibility, impartiality, efficiency, participation and humaneness, and a meaningful right to appeal. These twin principles and the elements that give them operational meaning form the core of our administrative justice perspective.

5

BUILDING JUST
ORGANIZATIONS

Just as we recognize the need for public organizations to devise ways to increase efficiency and economy,
we also need to consider how they can better "institutionalize" the justice norms that were described in Chapter Four.
How can the structures, processes, and technologies of public
organizations best be used to promote justice in administrative decision making? Exploring this question is the primary
aim of this chapter.

A useful beginning is to recall that a concern for justice
is a deeply rooted characteristic of public organizations in the
United States. As we saw in Chapter One, its origin can be
traced to our founding as a nation and is expressed most
clearly in our constitutional framework, which provides for a
government in which power is diffused and constrained by a
system of checks and balances. As a result, James Q. Wilson
(1989) says, we have a government that emphasizes due process over outcome and equity over efficiency. The fundamental characteristics of the bureaucratic organization, which
provide some of the essential prerequisites for justice in public
organizations, reinforce this basic attribute of our constitutional order.

This chapter begins with an examination of the elements of the bureaucratic form of organization that are
intended to foster justice and fair treatment. This is followed

by an exploration of some obstacles to attaining justice, obstacles commonly found in bureaucratic organizations. We then consider the role that both formal and informal culture systems play in establishing and maintaining justice norms in public organizations. Our purpose here is not to provide an action plan or strategy but rather to stimulate fresh ways of thinking about administrative justice in public organizations.

The Case for Bureaucracy

The relationship between bureaucracy and administrative justice is complex. Some attributes of bureaucracy promote fair treatment or justice, while others may inhibit its realization. Although noted primarily as a vehicle for efficiency and economy, the classic model of bureaucracy also incorporates elements that are intended to promote justice. Bureaucracy (rational-legal authority) promotes justice principally by requiring that the bureaucracy's actions be grounded in rules that have been established by proper procedures and are applied equally.

For example, by reducing rules to writing, bureaucracy promotes certainty, uniformity, and consistency in decision making and helps to curb arbitrary action. The importance of written rules is underscored when we consider that rules, whether written or unwritten, are always present in organizations. When they are not written, rules are likely to exist in the form of informal expectations and prohibitions. These tacit rules are unfair by definition because of the difficulty involved in discovering them (Perrow, 1986, pp. 23-28). To be regarded as fair, rules must be open, known, and clear. This is essential not only for protecting the rights of those to whom the rules apply but also so that they can be subject to debate, challenge, and change when they prove to be ineffective or even harmful.

Suppose an implicit rule in a city housing agency is that preferential treatment be given to white couples who apply for an apartment in a senior citizen housing complex that has a waiting list. Minority applicants not only have less chance to obtain an apartment than do nonminorities but they have little possibility for remedy because they do even not know that the race-based decision rule exists. By putting rules in writing, bureaucracy makes them explicit, fixed, and knowable.

Written rules assist in ensuring fair treatment in several tangible ways. First, they are a permanent record of agency policy decisions, promoting consistency in decision making by serving as a guide for decision makers. Second, when they are open and comprehensible, rules can provide meaningful access to the bureaucracy's decision process to those who may be affected by government actions. Third, written rules help decision makers make appropriate distinctions between cases or claims by delineating which are relevant (and irrelevant) similarities and differences. In the above illustration, race ought not to be a factor in assessing applications for subsidized senior citizen housing, but family income may be an appropriate consideration in determining an applicant's eligibility. Fourth, written rules constitute a set of standards against which to judge the actions of administrators. They provide the basis for appeal of administrators' decisions that are felt to be incorrect or unfair, for agency and external monitoring of administrative actions to ensure conformity to governing policy, and for assessment of the policy's effectiveness.

Other elements of bureaucracy similarly help to foster justice in administrative decision making. *Impersonality* seeks to assure that the rules will be applied impartially, without any favoritism or bias. *Technical knowledge* promotes accuracy and the proper exercise of discretionary authority, as technical expertise encompasses knowledge of the relevant policies, rules, and procedures as well as the substantive issues to be decided. Each office or position has an explicitly defined *sphere of competence*, limiting the bureaucrat's authority and ensuring the ability to act within that sphere. *Hierarchically structured authority* provides an avenue for correction of errors in decision making and redress of grievances. It also ensures that individual bureaucrats are held accountable to policymakers and, ultimately, the public.

An interesting way in which bureaucracy promotes justice can be found in the area of employee selection. Consider the agency director who hires one of the political party "faithful" for a position for which he clearly is unqualified. Perrow (1986) refers to this as "particularism," by which he means choosing an employee using criteria that are not relevant to organizational purposes, which is unjust because it is a misallocation of public resources (Perrow, 1986, pp. 8–10, 15). Viewed in terms of our criteria for just decision making, it also fails to meet the rational relationship test as well as the efficiency standard. Bureaucracy reduces the influence of particularism through its emphasis upon written rules, neutrality, and technical competence. Bureaucracy also furthers justice by lessening the abuse of their official position by people of high organizational status. As Perrow expresses the problem: "People tend to act as if they owned their positions; they use them to generate income, status, and other things that rightfully belong to the organization" (Perrow, 1986, p. 17).

The government official who spends public funds for a lavish redecorating of his office, who accepts privileged treatment from a potential favor seeker, or who steers an agency contract to an old friend is acting as though the office is an entitlement and not a public trust. He also violates our standards of justice, including the rational relationship test, the formal principle of justice, and the discretionary authority criterion, respectively. Bureaucracy has made great progress in curbing abuses of position by reducing the gap between an individual's contributions to the organization and the inducements necessary to retain him and to keep him performing effectively (Perrow, 1986, p. 17).

Strengthening the elements of the bureaucratic organization that promote justice is doubly important because of bureaucracy's great potential for injustice, which is disturbing precisely because the bureaucracy is such an effective means for achieving goals. Those who control the bureaucratic organization have a superb tool for achieving their ends (Perrow, 1986). When their aims are unjust, bureaucratic means will make their control that much more harmful.

Barriers to Organizational Justice

Among the barriers to fully institutionalizing justice in public organizations are several potentially harmful tendencies shared by all bureaucratic organizations. For example, with the exception of technical rationality norms, managers typically do not think of their organization's functioning in normative terms (Amy, 1987a). The challenge lies in inculcating justice norms in organizations so that these norms are accepted as key decision premises. Rohr (1978) argues that this becomes more difficult with each passing year as technical rationality continues to be accepted as the dominant norm governing decision making.

Critics have identified four major bureaucratic dysfunctions or "pathologies" in which the essential elements of bureaucracy (for example, rules, specialization) lead to inefficiency rather than efficiency. These dysfunctions are "trained incapacity," a dual system of authority, the "rigidity cycle," and "goal displacement" (March and Simon, 1958). In addition to leading to inefficiency, these bureaucratic dysfunctions create barriers to achieving justice.

By training its employees in very narrow, specialized areas, bureaucracy creates personnel with a "trained incapacity" to see beyond the special requirements of their own jobs. Lacking a broader understanding of the organization, the typical bureaucrat is unable to respond effectively when confronted by a new or unique situation that is not part of his narrowly defined scope of authority (Merton, 1949).

The dual system of authority refers to the inevitable conflict between knowledge-based and hierarchy-based authority in bureaucracy. The subordinate, with his specialized knowledge that the superior lacks, must defer to the superior's legitimate hierarchical authority. The superior, in turn, has the authority and responsibility to decide but lacks the specialized knowledge needed to exercise authority responsibly.

The "rigidity cycle" refers to the tendency of bureaucrats to justify their behavior through hierarchy and rules. The tendency for rule-bound behavior is a response to bureaucracy's managerial style—hierarchical, impersonal, and standardized. It is most pronounced when the bureaucracy (and the individual bureaucrat) experience uncertainty or feel threatened, so that the existing rules are enforced, new rules are promulgated, and hierarchical authority is stressed. Thus a cycle is set in motion in which the bureaucracy's response to problems produced in part by inflexibility is greater emphasis on hierarchy and rules, and the cycle of rigidity plays out.

The fourth bureaucratic dysfunction is what Robert Merton (1949) has termed "goal displacement." Closely related to the rigidity cycle, goal displacement refers to the tendency in organizations to treat rule compliance as an end in itself, even when the rule no longer serves as an effective means to a policy end, or the policy end is no longer a priority. Goal displacement is a pernicious tendency, as it results in attention and resources being shifted from achievement of legitimate policy objectives. An extreme example of goal displacement, writes Merton (1949, p. 155), "is the bureaucratic virtuoso, who never forgets a single rule binding his action and hence is unable to assist many of his clients."

These four bureaucratic pathologies have direct and significant implications for administrative justice. They go well beyond the justice problems created by inefficiency and failure to achieve legitimate policy goals. For example, each dysfunction makes it less likely that persons interacting with a bureaucratic agent will receive the individualized treatment that the formal principle of justice requires.

Another general barrier to achieving justice in bureaucratic organizations is what Irving Janis (1982) calls "groupthink." This occurs in decision groups when members forego contributing to a decision or challenging the group's decisions because they are reluctant to create conflict or they fear disturbing the group's cohesiveness. Groupthink can result in injustice as it produces decisions that defer to the interests of the group, overlooking the rights of individuals and the public interest.

Three additional tendencies of bureaucratic organizations merit reference here. The first is the propensity toward sacrificing the rights of the individual for some aggregate utility (that is, when the end overshadows the means). The second relates to the bureaucracy's tendency toward fragmentation of responsibility. The third is the result of structuring decision making so that no one person has responsibility for the decision and its consequences.

The tendency for bureaucracy to focus on aggregate utility to the neglect of the individual goes beyond the need to balance the competing demands of individual and aggregate justice. What is problematic is bureaucracy's tendency to rationalize disregard of individual rights by asserting a larger social utility. Two recent examples of injustices caused by the willingness of the bureaucracy to disregard individual rights are the Department of Energy's use of the cloak of "national security" to keep health risk information from persons who live near atomic weapons plants and the Social Security Administration's pressure on field staff to terminate Supplemental Security Income claimants as a way to cut program costs.

The second tendency, fragmented responsibility, may leave the individual administrator with insufficient discretionary authority to carry out his duties. When this occurs the likelihood of unjust actions increases, typically as a consequence of a policy or rule being applied inappropriately. In these cases the formal principle of justice is violated. Such severe constraints on discretionary authority also lead to the media stories of bureaucratic bungling that we have all seen and found amusing and exasperating.

A third harmful tendency is the structuring of decision making so that responsibility is fragmented: So many persons have responsibility for accomplishing parts of a given task that no one has sufficient responsibility to get the job done. In cases where decision-making authority is unclear, or when authority is multiple and overlapping, decisions may be seen as simply emerging as a result of the inexorable workings of the bureaucratic process (Tong, 1987). The danger is that justice concerns will fall between the cracks and there will be no voice for justice.

Environmental pressures also act as barriers to achieving organizational justice, especially likely to be the case when the organization operates in a resource environment that is highly competitive or is resource-poor. Intense competition for resources is typically associated with heavy workloads that often lead to acceptance of a norm of "cutting corners" to get things done, inadequate attention to policy objectives, a passive/reactive mode of agency operation (crisis management), and other coping strategies likely to result in the agency's ignoring justice issues. In such overburdened organizations, it can be especially difficult to secure the needed commitment for making significant changes, particularly when they relate to the more abstract values of justice and fairness.

Conversely, a resource-rich organization may overlook justice concerns, especially when an agency is under pressure to keep funds or projects moving through the "pipeline." This seems to be a root problem in the operation of the housing voucher program of the Department of Housing and Urban Development (HUD), which was created to give a cash subsidy to poor people so they could choose their own rental housing. Beginning in 1987, HUD regional offices came under pressure from Washington to make the voucher program succeed. Each regional office was given quotas and told to distribute their rent subsidies as quickly as possible. The quota for HUD's New York regional office in fiscal year 1987 was 12,000 vouchers. When the program proved difficult to launch in New York City, regional HUD officials pressured city housing officials to use all of their allotted program funds or risk losing the monies. In response, and with HUD approval, the New York City Department of Housing and Urban Development registered many ineligible families for the program. Nearly 600 families already living in subsidized housing received a double subsidy, a windfall that totals $2 million each year. As a result of the pressure to make the voucher program "work," a program targeted toward assisting poor families to find adequate housing became a boon for many families who already were receiving government housing subsidies (Winerip, 1989).

Finally, we need to recognize that in every organization there are strong forces at work that limit its capacity to change. James Q. Wilson observed that all organizations resist change and that government organizations in particular are averse to risk because they are so enmeshed in a set of constraints that any change is likely to antagonize an important constituency (Wilson, 1989). Unless there is scandal or a change of top leadership, it can be difficult to overhaul existing organizational policies, rules, and practices, even when they may be outmoded, ineffective, or harmful. Resistance to change makes it difficult to institutionalize justice when the requirements run counter to well-established formal and informal system practices (Kaufman, 1977).

Justice Facilitators

As the preceding discussion amply illustrates, many factors constrain a public organization's ability to institutionalize the principles of administrative justice. At the same time, public organizations also possess a number of attributes that help to create a climate that is supportive of justice values. Three common attributes of public organizations stand out as examples of "building blocks" for institutionalizing justice.

First, contemporary public organizations have already been conditioned to think in terms of justice values, in part owing to social equity pressures (for example, affirmative action) and to the demands of the due process explosion. Judicial review of administrative actions, including changing standards of personal liability, have sensitized administrators to issues of individual rights. More basically, public organizations are grounded in law and the Constitution. As a result, bureaucrats have considerable practical experience in interpreting judicial and legislative actions as well as in responding to their demands.

Moreover, in part as a result of the due process explosion and other environmental pressures, most government agencies have in place the basic elements of an administrative justice system. These include considerable experience in providing a variety of mandated hearings, as well as in employing employee grievance procedures and other dispute resolution systems. For example, many public agencies have had to devise means for meeting legislative requirements providing for public hearings to allow comment on proposed policy and rule changes.

Public organizations have even greater experience with the grievance procedure, which traditionally has been viewed as the means for everyday administration of the collective bargaining agreement. More recently the grievance procedure has been recognized for its importance as a means for ensuring procedural justice in the workplace, especially where it is not part of a collective bargaining agreement. It provides an opportunity for employees to seek redress of an improper or unfair action by the employer.

The typical grievance procedure includes the key elements of procedural due process, including notice, a neutral and impartial decision maker, evidentiary standards, opportunity to present one's side of the story, a decision that is on the record and grounded in the provisions of the collective bargaining agreement (that is, "in law"), a route of appeal, and so on. It also serves as a means of employee voice in the workplace, enabling workers to have a say in organizational decisions that affect them. Through the grievance procedure, managers and employees alike have direct experience with many of the basic principles of administrative justice in a forum that is the type of informal adjudicatory decision process envisioned by Judge Friendly and other due process scholars as "some kind of hearing."

Second, bureaucracy's expertise lies in implementation, in harnessing organizational resources to achieve predetermined objectives. Once the decision is made to focus on justice as a key organizational objective, the bureaucracy can apply its considerable skill and energy to achieving results. Were it given the objective of designing and operating a public organization that met standards of administrative justice, the bureaucracy could draw upon a wealth of technical expertise to achieve that objective.

For example, public organizations invest considerable resources in efforts to improve internal operations and delivery of services, including periodic reorganization of offices and functions. A recurring debate within organizations concerns the relative merits of centralization versus decentralization. The debate typically focuses primarily on questions of efficiency and effectiveness. When we add the value of justice to the equation, a new set of issues arises. For example, a primary concern will be the trade-off between the advantages of greater equality of treatment, consistency, quality control, and accountability offered by centralization and the advantages of decentralization, which include greater responsiveness, timeliness, sensitivity to those whom the bureaucracy serves, and ability to tailor policies and rules to individual needs (the formal principle of justice).

Take the case of a county health services agency whose mission is to provide a variety of prenatal services to women. By locating the services at the county's central offices, the agency can achieve economies of scale, provide each client with more extensive and specialized services, and have readier access to other county agencies, as well as to county officials. Agency centralization also may create hardships for clients, however, especially those for whom transportation to the county center is difficult or costly. Further, aggregating client services at a central location may mean that women seeking prenatal services may receive less individual attention, have less follow-up contact with caseworkers, and generally risk falling between the cracks of the system.

Decentralizing the prenatal program into storefront walk-in centers may enable the agency to reach greater numbers of women in need of prenatal services, at less burden to them and in their own, familiar neighborhood settings. Services may be more personalized, with continuity of caseworker assignment and greater attention to the unique service needs of each client. This individualized attention may better meet the requirements of the formal principle of justice. Conversely, because there is less opportunity for central monitoring and accountability, it also raises the prospect of wide variations in decision standards on questions such as eligibility, type and level of services to be provided, and so on.

Finally, a fundamental attribute of bureaucracy is its capacity for monitoring and control. Public agencies have considerable experience with a wide variety of instruments to ensure accountability, ranging from quality assurance mechanisms geared toward correcting systemic problems to various means to ensure accountability of individuals. Although many are not typically viewed explicitly in justice terms, they provide an excellent way to ensure accountability to justice standards. These accountability instruments include standard management tools such as employee supervision, budgetary review, internal auditing, and reporting systems. Agencies also can make use of external sources of information and performance feedback, such as advisory committees, public hearings, and citizen polls. In justice terms, this promotes accuracy by expanding the base of information for decision making, provides access and voice to affected groups, and increases the likelihood that administrative decisions will serve client interests rather than those of the agency.

Among the many other accountability tools are efforts to protect and encourage whistle-blowing; agency "hotlines" for fraud, waste, and abuse; and the agency office of inspector general. These tools are typically viewed narrowly as a means to curb illegality and corruption in public agencies, but they also serve justice by providing early warning signs and feedback on the effectiveness of policies and programs.

Quality Assurance in Adjudicative Decision Making. The linkage between quality assurance monitoring and the provision of administrative justice is especially relevant for agencies involved in claims management. As Jerry Mashaw (1974) notes, administrative justice in claims administration is concerned with the assurance of accuracy, fairness, and timeliness in agency adjudication of claims. Mashaw (1974, p. 772) uses the term "adjudication" more broadly than the formal trial-type proceeding typically called to mind by the term. In the social welfare claims setting, adjudication refers to any determination of eligibility or amount of benefits to be received, at any stage in the process. In essence, Mashaw is saying that decisions are just when the rules are applied properly: The correct benefits are received by those who qualify, and those who are not entitled to benefits under the rules do not receive them. Further, the decisions must be timely, that is, made within a reasonable or a statutorily prescribed period of time after the claim is presented.

Even a cursory glance at Mashaw's definitions makes it clear that legal safeguards of due process are insufficient to ensure justice. For this reason, Mashaw calls attention to the "managerial side of due process," especially the concept of quality assurance. Establishing a quality assurance system for due process protections requires the development of standards and methods for the evaluation of accuracy, timeliness, and fairness in claims adjudications. This involves ongoing review of decisions for correction of fact-finding errors and application of relevant program policy, establishing a system of appeals, and setting standards for performance (for example: How many decision errors are too many?). Evaluating fairness also must encompass the process elements of the decision-making system, the procedures and routines that are necessary for claims adjudication. These include adequacy of case development, explanation of the bases for decisions, notice to claimants of administrative actions, and explanations of opportunities for appeal.

Ensuring timeliness is less problematic than accuracy and fairness, in part because timeliness lends itself to standard setting, reporting, and quantitative expression. Further, agencies typically collect data relevant to timeliness as part of the ongoing system of performance evaluation, for allocation of staff, and for budgetary purposes. For example, Mashaw reports a Social Security Administration "man-hour" standard for adjudicating an initial disability claim, as well as an overall timeliness standard for processing claims. While timeliness clearly is of critical importance in claims adjudication, efficiency standards may create problems as well. Pressures to meet timeliness standards may result in poor decision making in individual cases. These kinds of problems can be addressed through review of the quality of decision making and by designing monitoring systems to include data that will enable the agency to discover incidents of "creaming" of easy cases and other negative effects of efforts to meet timeliness objectives.

The Role of Organizational Culture

The concept of organizational culture can be a useful tool for understanding the relationship between organizational behavior and justice. James W. Davis, Jr. (1974, p. 1) defines organizational culture as "[t]he pattern of shared beliefs and values that gives the members of an institution meaning, and provides them with the rules for behavior in their organization." It serves as the social or normative glue that holds the organization together and also serves as an organizational control system, both prescribing and prohibiting certain behaviors.

The existing culture of an organization can be supportive of justice values or in opposition to them. In the latter case, the organization's cultural norms actually may lead members to behave unjustly when as individuals they would not do so. We can see this harmful effect in many ways.

The power that cultural norms wield is especially evident in the socialization of new employees. Newcomers to organizations often face considerable pressure to conform to existing workplace norms, which may be formal and officially sanctioned or informal and based in the work group. Informal norms are especially important for institutionalizing justice when they are contrary to the organization's desired standards of behavior, whether they result in minor violations of work rules or official misconduct. For example, a new social welfare agency caseworker may be told by his co-workers that he should meet his monthly production quota by "creaming" benefits claims, that is, giving priority to applications that are easy to process. Violation of the agency's policy to give priority to applicants in most immediate need is explained away: "Skirting the rules is the only way to get the numbers that you need to keep the bosses happy." As a result, claimants whose applications need attention are shunted aside until the caseworker has some "free" time.

What is surprising at first blush is how readily employees will accept instructions to act in ways that conflict with their personal values or standards of conduct. For most individuals, this is possible because we follow different norms for different contexts. By segmenting our values, we are able to accept as appropriate in the workplace many kinds of behavior that would be unacceptable in another setting, such as in our family or among close friends. We can say to ourselves, "it's part of the job" and, therefore, "it's not really *me*" who is behaving in this unacceptable way, thereby reducing the dissonance that we might perceive between differing standards of conduct. An interesting variant of this dissonance-reducing reasoning is represented by Adolph Eichmann's famous defense plea when he was on trial for his role in the Nazi Holocaust: "I was only obeying orders."

Patterns of organizational decision making are established and maintained by both the formal and informal cultural systems of the organization. The relevant elements of the formal system include leadership, structure and policies, technology, reward systems, recruitment and selection, orientation and training program, and operating decision premises. The informal systems include norms, heroes and myths, rites and rituals, socialization, and stories and language.

Formal Organizational Systems. The impact of *leadership* on organizational decision making is difficult to assess. Some argue that leaders are the primary sources and transmitters of organizational culture (Davis, 1974), while others believe that leadership and decision patterns are created and shaped more by the values of the organization than by its leaders. Still, top organizational executives are seen as personifying the values of the organization, and they serve as role models for others to observe and follow.

Chester Barnard (1938) identified a fundamental requirement for organizational leadership when he said: "The inculcation of belief in the real existence of a common purpose is an essential executive function" (p. 87). There must be at least a minimal degree of "shared vision" of the organization's purpose.

What is the proper role of organizational leaders in institutionalizing justice in their organizations? In his classic study of leadership in administration, Phillip Selznick (1957, pp. 62–63) identified these essential functions:

1. The definition of institutional mission and role
2. The institutional embodiment of purpose
3. The defense of institutional integrity
4. The ordering of internal conflict

This involves setting goals, shaping the character of the organization, maintaining its values and distinctive identity, and managing internal conflict. Selznick emphasized the role of the leader in "organizational character formation." He argued that the leader makes critical policy decisions that influence the organization's development. These policies can be translated into guiding principles to be instilled in personnel through orientation and training programs and reinforced through the organizational reward system. In addition, the leader can recruit personnel who are more likely to fit in with his or her vision of the organization. The leader also serves as the organization's chief spokesperson and principal role model, the embodiment of the organization's mission and values.

The *formal structure* of an organization influences its system of values and the behavior of its personnel. For example, individual action is inhibited in an organizational system in which strict hierarchical relationships prevail, where duties are defined narrowly, and in which observing the chain of command is of paramount importance. In such a segmented system, individual decision makers are likely to be isolated.

The formal structure leads them to view problems narrowly and to take responsibility only for their limited, compartmentalized actions. Rosabeth Moss Kanter (1978) suggests that one way to break down these barriers is through integrative mechanisms and identification with the whole organization. This encourages decision makers to treat problems as wholes and to consider the wider implications of their actions.

Two specific ways organizational structure can influence decision making are through definition of authority relationships and attribution of responsibility for the consequences of actions. First, legitimate authority is an accepted tenet in public organizations. Individuals are expected to carry out the orders of those with legitimate authority, even when those orders are contrary to the subordinate's own judgment of what should be done. Second, the organization's formal structure may serve to diffuse responsibility. One way it does this is by promoting external definitions of employee responsibility that are based on formal role definitions, hierarchy, and authority, which reduces the individual's formal capacity (and willingness) to assume responsibility. Take the case of a manager who expresses concern for his employees when he learns of a hazardous condition in the workplace. The manager might be told by his superior that higher authorities in the organization are aware of the situation and will take steps to remedy the problem. At this stage the manager may feel that he has "done his duty" and has no further responsibility, even when the organization does not respond and the problem goes uncorrected. If he chooses to pursue the matter, he may be dissuaded by his superiors and others on the grounds that it is not his responsibility.

Another way that public organizations can encourage justice in decision making is by making the concern for justice a necessary and explicit part of formal organizational *policies* and *rules*. The more explicitly justice concerns are incorporated in policies and rules, the greater will be their likely impact. For example, performance appraisal systems are more likely to be viewed as fair when they involve employees in establishing appraisal standards, developing appraisal instruments, setting performance objectives, and assessing outcomes; when they link job performance to merit increases, promotions, and other rewards; and when they provide a channel for appeal of disputed ratings.

Increasingly, *codes of ethical conduct* act as a formal policy tool to guide organizational members' behavior. Although existing research evidence on the effectiveness of ethics codes is mixed, it suggests that where ethical codes are effective in guiding behavior, they are likely to reflect an existing organizational culture that supports ethical conduct. Effective ethics codes are seen as more than window dressing. The organization's *reward system* influences the behavior of its members and also has important symbolic value. By using merit increases, promotions, and other inducements to reward those who contribute to the goal of justice, management sends a message to organizational members than justice is valued and that the resources will be allocated in support of its achievement. Conversely, when the organization does not reward just behavior, it sends a message to employees that justice really is not very important.

The organization also can seek to cultivate justice values through its *recruitment* and *selection* process. At a minimum criteria relating to justice include fair treatment in recruiting and hiring persons, but they also include seeking to bring into the organization persons who have a concern for justice.

Orientation and training programs can communicate the importance of justice values to employees. Beginning with the orientation for new employees, public organizations can strive to instill in their employees a sensitivity to justice concerns. Training programs can be especially useful in providing guidance on justice as a criterion in decision making. Increasingly in recent years, for example, public-sector organizations have offered ethics training as part of their management development programs, programs that can be useful tools for managers to develop their own justice-centered frame of reference. Through in-service training in justice values, the organization not only offers specific skills to managers but also communicates that justice is an important organizational value to be given weight in administrative decision making.

Similarly, organizational *technologies* can be harnessed to enhance justice as well as efficiency. For example, performance monitoring systems can be structured to include data that serve as justice performance indicators. These could include standard measures of efficiency, but they also would contain data useful for monitoring decision accuracy and consistency, conformity to policy and rules, perceptions of fair treatment, and so on.

Informal Organizational Systems. Institutionalizing justice as a normative premise in public organizations also requires working with informal organizational systems, particularly through the use of exemplars based on the heroes, rituals, and stories that are an important part of the life of all organizations.

Heroes are symbolic figures who personify the organization's values and set standards for members by serving as models for desired behaviors. These heroes may no longer even be present in the organization, but stories about their values and achievements continue to influence daily behavior in the organization. The influence of charismatic leaders such as William Ruckleshaus in his two tours at the helm of the U.S. Environmental Protection Agency and Sargent Shriver at the Peace Corps endures in these agencies long after the end of their tenure. A hero's influence may also extend well beyond the organization, inspiring untold numbers of persons.

Rites and *rituals* are expressive events that give public recognition to appropriate behavior, conveying symbolically what the organization wants its members to do and how it expects them to do it (Deal and Kennedy, 1984). Rituals also provide opportunities to celebrate the organization's culture. In doing so, they also remind us of our common organizational purposes, rejuvenate us, and lead us to renew our commitment to the organization. Although they typically foster norms of productivity and loyalty to the organization, rituals also can reinforce a shared commitment to justice as an organizational goal.

One ritual we have all participated in at one time or another is the retirement dinner, a ceremony that expresses the value placed on loyalty to the organization. It also provides the opportunity to highlight the retiree's career in terms of important organizational values. Another common organizational ritual is the awards ceremony, where tribute is paid to employees for their length of service, some meritorious achievement, or another form of contribution to the organization. Similar rituals can be created to recognize and honor individuals who have demonstrated a commitment to justice, to celebrate hard-won organizational victories or successes, and to commemorate heroes and past achievements.

Certain management rituals also can reinforce the organization's concern for justice. Periodic planning meetings, program review sessions, or staff retreats provide an opportunity to underscore and reinforce justice values. Similarly, managers can use their role as mentors to subordinates to instill in them justice values.

Much of the *socialization* process in organizations is conducted informally by role models such as superiors or more experienced peers. This process includes socialization regarding desirable and undesirable behavior. Particularly susceptible to socialization influences are those entering new organizational situations, such as newly hired persons and individuals transferring from one part of the organization to another. For example, in every organization new employees will be exposed to conduct that is unethical or otherwise undesirable. A classic example is that of the rookie patrolman assigned to a seasoned officer, who learns on the first day on the beat that it is permissible to accept a free meal at a neighborhood restaurant or to overlook a tavern's liquor law violations in return for a contribution to the "widows and orphans fund." Once the new patrolman has been socialized into this informal set of undesirable organizational norms, it will be difficult to redefine the job to negate their influence. In contrast, the mentor or role model may emphasize justice concerns, as well as broader positive values such as the importance of one's personal and professional integrity.

Another extremely important way to transmit and keep justice values alive is through the *informal communication network*. Organizational myths, sagas, and stories, which are accounts of events drawn from the organization's history, explain and give meaning to an organizational culture. The characters in the story are members of the organization and the moral of the story expresses the organization's values. An example is the retelling of how a deserving program was saved from the budget cutters' ax through the valiant efforts of a dedicated staff, or the successful launching of a controversial new program despite seemingly insurmountable obstacles. Of course, informal storytelling also may be destructive of justice values, especially when the moral of the story is that unjust behavior is accepted or even encouraged. There is a strong signal about the culture of an organization when the most often retold stories are of the clever manager who "got around" the civil service rules to hire and promote his friends, or who succeeded in "beating" the agency's affirmative action system, or who managed to "skirt the rules" to divert program funds toward unintended purposes.

Even the *language* that we use conveys the organization's operative values to its members and those whom it serves. All organizations employ specialized language to facilitate internal communications; it is an integral element in both the formal and informal organizational systems. Indeed, it is difficult to imagine how questions of justice in public organizations could be discussed without an appropriate vocabulary. Consider just three of the terms (and their special meanings) that were introduced in Chapter Four: "policy as rule," "rational relationship test," and "transparency." This special vocabulary can be developed through both formal and informal organizational systems (for example, orientation and training programs, mentoring, rituals and stories).

We must remember, however, that specialized language also may have negative effects as well. In the formal communication system, it can take the form of "bureaucratese," the often arcane language of government agencies that can be so maddening to the uninitiated. Those brave souls who enter the bureaucrat's world risk being overwhelmed by seemingly indecipherable acronyms, jargon, and garbled prose. Perhaps most pernicious is "doublespeak," that form of miscommunication in which budget cuts are referred to as "advanced downward adjustments," potholes in the road become "pavement deficiencies," and prisoners no longer are placed in solitary confinement but in "individual behavior adjustment units."

Informal communications may include specialized vocabulary that helps to lighten stressful work situations or to maintain a distance between agency employees and the various stakeholders with whom they interact. This is especially likely to occur in high-stress, burnout work settings. Thus, staff in pediatric burn wards may refer to their charges as "crispy critters," while in many psychiatric wards the patients are "the zombies." As these two illustrations suggest, language can lay the groundwork for injustice by dehumanizing a decision situation, which can make an unjust act easier to commit, excuse, and accept. On the other hand, for the organization's clients, the language used in communicating about and with those whom the bureaucracy serves can further justice and be an important element in perceptions of fair treatment, self-respect, and dignity. For example, agency practice should encourage probation officers to refer to those under their supervision as clients and caseworkers at a shelter for the homeless to call its patrons guests.

Building a Justice-Centered Organizational Culture

Institutionalizing justice in public organizations requires creating and sustaining an organizational culture that provides and reinforces justice-centered norms of decision behavior. Experience with planned change efforts in a variety of organization settings teaches us that organizational change can be a difficult, time-consuming, and expensive undertaking.

Planned change efforts must overcome the pervasive human tendency to want to conserve and protect existing organizational systems. Fortunately, public organizations already possess many of the attributes necessary for creating and sustaining a justice-centered culture. We suggested several important attributes of bureaucracy earlier in this chapter.

We also need to keep in mind that organizational culture is functional. The existing cultural practices of every bureaucracy have developed as part of adaptation to circumstances in its environment. Cultural elements that decrease the bureaucracy's survival chances are not likely to persist. Significant threats or challenges from the environment require cultures to change; for example, a major event or incident in a public agency may pave the way for a reorientation of the organization's value system and practices. Organizations caught up in a scandal, or those faced with costly lawsuits, are prime candidates for major changes in organizational culture.

Even when significant threats or challenges from the environment do not confront bureaucracies, ongoing forces operating in the environment help to create a climate supportive of change. The past two decades witnessed an incredible amount of change in the operating environment of the typical public agency, including increased sensitization to the rights of individuals, demands by the public for greater openness and accountability, and the entry into the public service of large numbers of women, minorities, and persons who are handicapped. This environmental climate of change is likely to continue for the knowable future. These environmental forces can help to "unfreeze" many public organizations, preparing them for the changes needed to create and sustain justice-centered organizational cultures.

The organizational change literature suggests that any attempt at major change of an organization's culture requires a systemwide approach, taking both the formal and informal systems into account (Tichy, 1983). It also must be voluntary (Argyris, 1970). Without free-informed choice to participate, major planned change efforts are not likely to be effective and raise serious ethical issues.

Ethical concerns are especially important when trying to foster justice-centered values in public organizations; that is, one cannot build a just organizational system by means that do not respect the rights of individuals. This does not mean that public agencies are powerless to act without the voluntary cooperation of every civil servant. It does indicate, however, that agency leadership and management must be sensitive to the concerns of employees and involve them as participants in the planned change process, respecting their desire for a voice in agency decisions that affect them.

Further, successful change assumes that individuals in the organization are basically good and open to growth and change. Through culture change, organizational definitions of appropriate behavior can be transformed, thereby relieving pressures on employees to engage in behavior that does not meet administrative justice standards. Finally, the process of building a justice-centered organizational culture must be approached as a long-term effort; effective planned change can take many years.

In this chapter we suggested that institutionalizing justice in public organizations requires an understanding of their formal and informal systems. We also suggested that the institutionalization of justice is well under way in many public organization settings. Some of the elements of justice are part and parcel of the bureaucratic model, and others have been internalized as a result of court mandates and other environmental forces. By and large, however, justice is not embedded in organizational culture in any conscious, systematic way. To institutionalize justice in organizational decision making, the organization's cultural systems must be targeted in a long-term, capacity-building effort based upon justice values.

6

QUALITIES OF THE
JUST ADMINISTRATOR

Chapter Four presented the criteria for the making of just administrative decisions, and Chapter Five addressed the challenges to implementing such decisions in public organizations. A crucial area for discussion remains, one that critically affects the question of whether or not a system for just administrative decision making can be built. At the core of the just organization is an individual decision maker who, in the final analysis, will determine whether the guidelines are employed and whether the required organizational change will occur. Ultimately, the values, sensitivities, knowledge, skills, attitudes, and personal attributes of people within public organizations are essential to administrative justice.

What cognitive and affective qualities and skills does the administrative justice framework require of public managers? What attitudes and personal attributes serve the ends of justice? How might they be sought or applied? This chapter addresses such questions.

The Administrator's Dilemma

Lodged within a unique organizational culture having its own special perspective and needs, the public administrator who would be just must develop a way of looking at the world that has three overlapping and potentially conflicting perspectives. He must act on behalf of *the organization* that employs him, giving due regard to the organization's interests in survival, reputation, and effectiveness. He must serve the expectations of *citizens* he comes in contact with—clients, regulated parties, public employees—for responsive and fair treatment. Finally, he must attempt to maximize the policy goals of *political superiors* and the general public they represent.

Public administrators are far from being a homogeneous lot and they play a number of different roles, but their central and legitimizing responsibility is to implement public policy. Although they must get involved, their central function is not to be political leaders (as those for whom they work) or technical experts (as those whom they supervise). Once goals are established in law and are confirmed as a working premise at the top of the organization, each administrator on down the hierarchy can be expected to be proactive in developing the kind of rules and procedures that anticipate the needs of that policy and help to realize it.

Public administration ethics scholars tend to place most of the responsibility for ethical renewal upon the mid-level manager. But how should this be done? The command "to be ethical" provides, in and of itself, little guidance on how to make normative decisions. Denhardt is typical in insisting on the widest possible range of moral judgment for the administrator: "While it is possible to give the administrator some guidance as to what the appropriate moral principles ought to be, it is not possible to give such specific guidelines or to develop a sophisticated enough process for arriving at moral judgments to assure that the administrator will not have to rely ultimately upon an individual moral judgment" (1988, p. 113).

Rohr (1978) suggested that administrators inquire into "regime values," a fairly discrete set of values enunciated by the Supreme Court in their judicial opinions (property, equality, freedom, and so on) that reasonably thoughtful persons are capable of understanding, internalizing, and applying.

Cooper (1982) goes much further in giving practical guidance. He tells us that moral judgment is rooted in the individual administrator's various roles as citizen, organizational member, and thinking person, and he explicates these roles. Ethical responsibility, he reasons, flows from linking obligations of public participation, laws and policies, certain prescribed inner qualities (such as accepting ambiguity, cultivating courage, and possessing a sense of fairness), and accepting a "legitimate" organizational role (answerable to constitutional norms). In its totality, however, the difficulty of both understanding and applying the behaviors suggested by these roles is great.

Although helpful in our thinking about various aspects of what it means to be ethical, these guidelines do not add as much as we might like to Denhardt's call for individual moral judgment. In sum, the vagueness of these prescriptions prompts sympathy with the view expressed in a leading textbook of the field: "What is needed for the public administrator is a simple and operational conceptualization of the public interest that permits him to make a moral choice on the basis of rational thinking" (Henry, 1975, p. 40). This does not mean that the individual administrator will be able to shift personal responsibility for decisions or that by applying the conceptualization she will be able to avoid conflict with the organization's hierarchy.

The important question, then, is whether administrative justice provides greater guidance and more protection for the administrator than other prescriptions for ethical decision making. The mid-level manager, who may have little influence in what or how organizational goals are set, has an ethical responsibility to the organization and, further, is vulnerable to and dependent upon it. Although she theoretically has the legal discretion to act, she is severely restricted by these facts. She thus needs all the help she can get.

Consider the plight of the administrator who, convinced that justice requires a decision not supported by his organization's leadership and prepared mentally to make it, must nonetheless have the cooperation of other members of the organization to effectively implement the decision. If he is able to support his argument by demonstrating that his decision is consistent with public policy and treats all parties fairly, he is more likely to prevail than if he simply argues that his decision is morally correct.

Administrative justice attempts to direct the administrator's judgment according to more objective standards for ethical judgments. It does not go as far as most administrative ethics theories in arguing that individual responsibility must displace organizational responsibility. Justice imposes individual responsibility, but it is easier to shoulder because (1) it is relatively clear, (2) it is consistent with legitimate organization interests, (3) it has greater legitimacy than action upon a "morally justifiable ground," and (4) it recognizes the public manager's burden to serve public policy and citizen interests as well as organizational goals. By recognizing the manager's limited power base in the organization, it supports him in shouldering personal risk, although it does not totally shield him from attack.

General Demands of Administrative Justice

We will look closely in the latter part of this chapter at what public administrators do in their various and specific roles, but several things can be said about what applying the administrative justice framework requires of them as a general matter. Reviewing the criteria of a just administrative decision and exploring the challenges of institutionalizing justice in the public organizational context expose us to the need for a set of knowledge and cognitive skills, attitudes, and attributes to nurture and sustain the administrator who would be just.

Knowledge and Cognitive Skills

What should a manager know to act justly? Perhaps at the top of the list should be the knowledge and tools that will allow him to know his role and responsibility in the constitutional system, to understand the sources of his discretionary authority, to be able to trace the making of public policy so as to understand its intent and content, and to understand the various processes by which government makes choices. Cognitive knowledge and skills should encompass an appreciation of the Constitution, facility in working with law, an assessment of the appropriateness of means, mastery of the essentials of due process, techniques of conflict management, and an understanding and an ability to work with various types of evidence.

Constitutionalism. To begin with, the just administrator must have a basic understanding of the principles embodied in the constitutional system. This obligation includes an appreciation of the Constitution as basic law; concepts of separation of powers and checks and balances among the legislative, executive, and judicial branches; the nature of federalism; the role of individual liberties and minority rights; and the underlying right of the electorate to shape and change law as well as the Constitution itself.

Associated with constitutionalism is a basic knowledge of policy process. To find the principle embedded in a policy, it is usually necessary to understand that it is the product of a political compromise. To understand the basis of the compromise entails an understanding of the positions and policy goals of the various stakeholders. Such knowledge may well enable the administrator to distinguish policy principles from rules that simply intend to assist in realizing the principle. Implicit in understanding the policy process is some knowledge of executive planning and budgeting, legislative and judicial processes, and the art and craft of resolving conflict.

Law. The rational pursuit of the principles embedded in public policies demands of administrators the ability to find and make sense of the law. Legislation and legislative history, judicial and attorney general opinions, executive orders and policy position statements emanating from executive staff and the appointed heads of administrative units, administrative regulations and adjudicative opinions should not be unfathomable mysteries but should be brought within the realm of the administrator's understanding. These are the tools he will need to discover the lawmaker's intent and to monitor whether others who interpret this intent have stayed on course.

In general, administrators should *not* study administrative law: the details of formal rulemaking and adjudication and the practices relating to judicial review of administrative action. An exception should be made for the essentials of administrative due process, which are described below. These principles can be mastered and applied in informal decision settings as well as in formal settings. Such knowledge should strengthen the administrator's hand in dealing with attorneys hired by organizational clients, regulated parties, and public employees.

Ability to Appraise Means in the Light of Ends. Beyond understanding the principles embodied in policy, the administrator must make a judgment about whether proposed administrative action is rationally related to the policy and whether it holds potential for unfair treatment of the persons or groups subject to the policy. For example, if it is proposed that a mental health facility conveniently located for use by clients be moved to an inconvenient area, and an examination of underlying policy reveals that mental health programs are designed to serve low-income persons, the administrator must decide whether the proposed decision works against the service principle envisioned by the policy, an equity issue that might escape an insensitive administrator's attention. In this situation, for example, the proposal can be seen as working an injustice on persons who were the intended beneficiaries of the policy in order to serve the interests of others (middle-class users or administrators themselves).

Due Process. All public administrators, regardless of their particular role, should acquire knowledge of the general requirements of due process. The basic elements of due process are developed by the courts and, once announced, protected by the Constitution. Due process consists of those procedural protections regarded by our society (as judged by the courts) as fundamental to fairness and traditional in our culture. The number and identity of the procedures to be applied vary with type and importance of the dispute and what has been thought to be traditionally fair in this situation.

These safeguards have been developed primarily with reference to judicial disputes, but they are applicable to formalized adjudication in the agencies as well. Most disputes in public administration, however, are informal and dealt with by ordinary public administrators, and the courts have had little to say about what procedures should be used in such a context. It is therefore incumbent upon public administration to spell out what fair or due process means in the informal setting.

From the public administrator's perspective, perhaps no better statement has been uttered about due process than this passage from Emmette Redford's writing.

> The subjection of man to administration is not new, and we can find in our traditional administrative law four primary principles for protection of the citizen before administration. They are notice, opportunity to be heard, decision without bias, and independent review. These four rudimentary principles of justice, asserted in some old areas of administration, supply the standards for a modern charter of constitutionalism in the relations of citizens to the powerful and pervasive modern administrative state. They cannot be implemented by law alone, and they do not meet all the needs for protection of the citizen. They cannot take the place of correction through political process, or of effective administrative organization and internal decision processes. But they are essential for protection of the rights of men before administration and for embodiment of the democratic ideal in administrative practice. They are guides for nonlegal (informal) as well as legal (formal) administrative practice (1969, p. 136).

Notice, opportunity to be heard, decision without bias, and independent review must be defined in the administrative context by administrators. Not only must these fundamental rights receive an administrative meaning but the legal profession's proper role in securing and defending these rights within the context of the informal administrative process must be carefully delineated. Administrators must then become zealous in ensuring the protection of citizens and employees in the exercise of these fundamental procedural rights.

In the more formal hearing settings where lawyers are present, administrators must develop the ability to distinguish advocate motives for securing fundamental rights from motives to delay the decision or secure special tactical advantage for the benefit of winning cases for clients. They might also be expected to complain when the procedures for asserting and protecting rights begin to get in the way of delivering rights to whole classes of citizens as a part of the public policy due them. This means that, although they are committed to guaranteeing fundamental rights, they have an obligation to point out to policymakers where the exercise of certain rights interferes with the objective of pursuing legitimate policy goals, so that the latter have the opportunity of changing the policy to serve both goals.

Conflict Management. Recent experimentation with managing conflicts through negotiation, arbitration, and mediation highlights the importance many governments at all levels place on finding alternatives to formal process. The reasons seem fairly obvious: Enormous costs—in dollars, delays, and decisions not responsive to the need for rational policy development—are associated with protracted trial-type hearings and legal maneuvering. Also, it may be easier and far cheaper to resolve a dispute in the early stages before it becomes an intractable situation where the parties commit themselves to positions from which they cannot gracefully retreat.

The just administrator has a responsibility to keep abreast of new methods, such as negotiated rulemaking, which hold potential for managing and resolving disputes that impede fair and efficient policy implementation. It would be a mistake, however, to assume that alternative dispute resolution (ADR) activities are an unalloyed helpmate to just administration. Factors favoring both justice and injustice operate *within* negotiation, arbitration, and mediation settings as well as in formal adjudication or, for that matter, any other mode of decision making. Unequal financial resources, political influence, organizational capacities, and skills of the stakeholder groups and their advocates play an important role in outcomes (Amy, 1987b). A party who will be affected by the outcome is likely to be adversely affected if not allowed to participate or participate fully. In face-to-face negotiations, the negotiation skills of the advocates for the various interests become critical. Relatively unsophisticated interests who have little experience and few resources to secure a competent negotiator or engage in careful fact-finding and strategy preparation are certainly disadvantaged.

In such a climate, just administration demands more from the administrator than simple facilitation. It requires taking an active role in balancing the scales as to effective participation, accuracy, transparency, and other criteria of procedural justice. Following the criteria of the administrative justice framework is the basic reference point, but to do so *in the context of negotiation,* administrators must know a good deal about the dynamics of the particular method employed.

The Nature of Evidence. "Getting at the truth" is done differently by lawyers, social scientists, and politicians, who differ in what they accept as facts and in what they accept as "proof." The rules for determining what is admissible in a court of law are explained partly by standards of logical relevance, but also they are affected by institutional and historical factors. Dear to the lawyer's heart, for example, is the notion that information that does not bear directly upon the case being tried should not be examined. Social scientists, on the other hand, pay attention to the scientific method and to the rules of mathematical probability. These concerns lead them to look at many similar cases to draw conclusions. Politicians' assessments of questions of fact turn heavily upon the identification of the values held by political interest groups and the intensity with which they are asserted. Data are sought that will be useful in predicting how certain positions will go down with blocks of potential voters.

Legal, social science, and political methods for discovering facts are suited to settling different kinds of disputes and making different kinds of decisions, differences that administrators need to study and appreciate to apply the right kind of fact-finding effort to each situation. These differences have obvious significance regarding the type of forum and decision mode that administrators should employ for making decisions.

Attitudes

In addition to a knowledge base and cognitive skills, the just administrator must be equipped with a set of attitudes to enable him or her to perceive and act upon a question of justice as it is presented in the administrative setting.

Predisposition to Client Interests Over Personal or Organizational Interests. A distinction should be drawn between a client group targeted by public policy to be served or favored and the client as an individual claimant. Most clientele groups within the administrative state develop a dependency upon the administrative agencies created and commanded to serve them. This dependency and the resulting vulnerability of the client give rise to moral claims of clients upon administrators (Goodin, 1985; Rosenbloom, 1983a). Recognizing this moral claim and developing such a predisposition should become the subject of systematic indoctrination and training in the just organization.

However, when the issue is whether an individual should be defined as a member of the client group, as when a person applies for public assistance eligibility, or when disputes arise relative to the amount or nature of government benefits, that person deserves no special treatment beyond the fair application of the rules. The social service agency has an obligation to think in terms of what will benefit those on public assistance, but it should not bend the rules to help those the policy does not clearly intend to help. A good illustration of what a social service agency administrator could do for the individual client beyond enforcing the guidelines would be to serve as a broker for the client in gaining alternative sources of community support.

A Sense of Reasonableness. In the obvious situations where the uniform application of a rule works an injustice in the particular case, just administrators should follow that part of the formal principle of justice that admonishes to "treat unlike cases differently in proportion to the ways in which they are different." Justice should point us in the direction of modifying or even ignoring rules to meet the needs of doing justice in the nonconforming case, but of doing so in uniform ways. If some OSHA inspectors write up as plant violations every case of wall-mounted fire extinguishers less than the required three feet above the floor, other OSHA inspectors ignore the height of extinguishers, and still others cite violations for extinguishers less than two feet above the floor but only verbally call the plant's manager's attention to extinguishers if they sit two to three feet above the floor, justice is not well served. To achieve justice in the aggregate, all rules that deserve to be modified should be modified in the same way in every case, and all rules that deserve not to be applied should not be applied in any case.

It is the role of the just administrator not only to apply the formal principle of justice but to identify patterns of circumstances and guide citizens and agency employees in the uniform nonapplication or modification of a rule. Such patterns can then be made the basis for a new rule that either writes an exception to the basic rule or replaces the old rule. To perform this function requires the mental attitude of not feeling bound to rules as a matter of course, of being willing to review rules in order to determine if they are logically related to achieving the policy goal. In short, managers should be encouraged to develop an attitude of reasonableness regarding the application of rules. A rule for which an exception cannot be developed scarcely exists. A pattern of circumstances that does not fit the intent of the rule may itself be fashioned into a subrule that dictates a different treatment than the general rule would provide.

A Sensitivity to Others' Feelings of Injustice. Just public administrators should be sensitive to what causes people to feel they have been treated unjustly. As discussed in Chapter Seven, the feeling of being treated unjustly arises from a sense of suffering either an absolute or relative deprivation, either as an individual or as a member of a group. Whether an actual injustice has *occurred* is, in a sense, not as relevant as whether injustice is *perceived.*

Assuming the possibility that every complaint, regardless of how poorly expressed, may bear within it the seeds of injustice is critical. Attentive listening and treatment to everyone protects the dignity of persons, citizens and aliens, who come into contact with the administrative world. Moreover, when perceived injustices are allowed to accumulate without a genuine effort to understand them and to assist when possible, the result is serious erosion of the agency's legitimacy.

Flexibility. Stephen Bailey (1965) described what he believed to be three essential mental attitudes in the ethical public administrator: a recognition of the moral ambiguity of all men and of all public policies, a recognition of the contextual forces that condition moral priorities in the public service, and a recognition of the paradoxes of procedures. All of these contribute to the general conclusion that the just administrator must be a person with a flexible mind.

Public managers should understand that ambiguity permeates virtually all decision situations in government. At the same time that we recognize that personal self-interest cannot be avoided in working out public decisions, we must accept the conflicting observation that "the very call to serve a larger public often evokes a degree of selflessness and nobility on the part of public servants beyond the capacity of cynics to recognize or to believe" (Bailey, 1965, p. 287). Rationalization merges with rationalism to blur motive. We can probably depend upon two things: First, any decision motivated by self-interest is aided by justifying it on a higher, moral ground; second, it is important to take self-interest into account when analyzing or predicting another's decision. "Likewise, there is a moral ambiguity in all public policy. But one mark of moral maturity is in the appreciation of the inevitability of untoward and often malignant effects of benign moral choices" (Bailey, 1965, p. 288). In this recognition is an acceptance of the fact that "an adequate response to any social evil contains the seeds of both predictable and unpredictable pathologies" (Bailey, 1965, p. 288). Having public assistance policies reduces hunger but promotes dependence, protecting wilderness areas protects wildlife but decreases economic opportunities, and so forth.

Harlan Cleveland tells us that one of the key requisites of a successful administrator is a tolerance for ambiguity (or "polyguity," since real executive problems are many-sided rather than "ambi-," which means two-sided). "If the inside of each organization can be described as a web of tensions, its outside relations—with clients, veto groups, banks, unions, special-interest associations, public agencies, and legislatures—can be seen as a larger tension system, with Public Executives at each switching station trying to bring people together with a view to taking a next step. The prizes go to those who can move toward their subjective human purposes by tolerating a high degree of polyguity in return for a maximum amount of action" (1972, p. 85).

Ambiguity is magnified as the decision ascends the organizational ladder. Contextual considerations become more complex. The difficulty of a junior official's task of deciding a dispute according to a rule pales in comparison to an agency head's more complex need to gauge legislative and media reaction.

Procedural requirements add an additional layer of paradox and tensions. On the positive side, as Justice Frankfurter said in *Malinski v. New York* (1945, p. 414): "[t]he history of American freedom is, in no small measure, the history of procedure." Procedural rules exist to promote openness, accuracy, and accountability in public decision making. But inept procedures get in the way of making rational decisions by causing them to be more expensive, more cumbersome, and slower than they need to be to serve policy goals.

The public servant who cannot recognize the paradoxes of procedures will be trapped by them. For in the case of procedures, he who deviates frequently is subversive, he who never deviates at all is lost, and he who tinkers with procedures without an understanding of substantive consequence is foolish (Bailey, 1965, p. 292).

Personal Attributes

Finally, certain personality characteristics are desirable in the makeup of the just administrator. Bailey (1965) speaks of the "operating virtues"—optimism, courage, and fairness—as essential moral qualities in public service.

Optimism is "the quality which enables man to face ambiguity and paradox without becoming immobilized" (Bailey, 1965, p. 293). Although it scarcely seems the prevailing mood in government beset by financial crisis and a dispirited public service, it is essential for administrators to believe that government can do justice and somehow make the world a better place.

Courage is needed to deal with the degree of ambiguity and paradox that pervades public decision making. It takes courage to face down pressures based on friendship or popular majorities or expert opinion. "Normally it takes less courage to deal impersonally with identifiable interest groups than with long-standing associates and colleagues upon whom one has depended over the years for affection and for professional and personal support" (Bailey, 1965, p. 293). Examples can be found in the case of administrators who must make promotion or merit pay decisions that affect subordinates they have worked with for many years, or in the case of government inspectors who work closely and frequently with those whom they regulate. A good example is the case of a Federal Aviation Administration inspector in Fargo, North Dakota, who asked for the arrest of a Northwest Airlines plane crew on its arrival in Minneapolis-St. Paul. Prior to the flight, he detained them on a tip that they had been drinking heavily, and while he was seeking instructions from local police, they took off with ninety-one passengers aboard. It would have been easier to have simply waited to see if the plane arrived safely, particularly in light of the fact that he had not smelled alcohol on their breath before they left the ground ("Northwest Pilots," 1990).

Legal counsel constantly inveighs public managers to avoid taking action that could risk liability. Threats of personal or agency legal liability lies in the air as likely consequences of not following their advice. Yet, the agency lawyer's role is different from the administrator's—the former is not responsible for the achievement of public policies. Lawyers tend by their training to be risk-averse and cautious. Mosher (1982) cautions governmental actors with broad decision responsibilities to avoid adopting the narrow view upon which professional judgments are based.

Because decisions made about public disputes inevitably cause pain to some, a basic part of courage in the public administrator is the courage to decide. Examples are decisions as diverse as allocating grant funds among cities for community development, or selecting an outsider to head a unit that includes internal candidates for the position, or determining which students to admit to an elite public university's graduate program.

Fairness, tempered with charity, is "the third and perhaps most essential moral quality needed in the public service" (Bailey, 1965, p. 296). This quality entails sensitivity to the needs and interests of all persons and groups affected by agency policies and programs. A fair mind is a mind that is not predisposed to reaching certain outcomes on the basis of prejudice or self-interest. Fair-mindedness means neutrality to both parties and policies, save only that the policies and beneficiaries that the law directs the agency to serve are of course given a special place.

Charity must supplement the objectivity required for fairness. According to Bailey, "Public servants are always faced with making decisions based upon both imperfect information and the inarticulate insinuations of self-interests into the decisional calculus. Charity is the virtue which compensates for inadequate information and for the subtle importunities of self in the making of judgments designed to be fair" (1965, p. 296). Fairness without charity shades into moral righteousness and tends to ignore the ambiguity of personal motives and policies.

Two things can be done to aid in seeing that administrators are equipped with the attributes we have discussed. First, both formal and informal structures and methods can encourage and reinforce them. On the formal side, organizational policies and practices can be developed that identify and highlight desired attributes, and organizational rewards can be designed to follow. More can be done in recruiting, selecting, and promoting. For instance, assessment centers can develop simulations that permit candidates for entry and promotions the opportunity to show how they would respond in specific situations in which fairness is pitted against hierarchical influence or interest group pressures.

Second, the organization can work at changing the "reference frames" of decision makers, the patterned ways people have of looking at the world. Administrators can be coaxed, trained, required, and otherwise prodded into taking new variables into account when they make decisions. They may not necessarily internalize justice-related attributes when doing so, but still they will be exposed to them and may develop appropriate habits. For example, the organization can train personnel staff not to ask questions that are not related to the position (marital status, sexual preference, and the like) when interviewing prospective employees.

The Multiple Justice Roles of Public Administrators

Beyond these general observations that apply to all public administrators, things can be said regarding the relationship of justice to each of several, specific public administrator roles. In the following pages, these common roles will be addressed: (1) adjudicator, (2) policymaker, (3) manager, (4) supervisor of professionals, (5) advocate, (6) public role model, and (7) consumer of goods and services.

Adjudicator. The role with perhaps the clearest implications for justice is that of dispute settler, or adjudicator. Adjudication is a decision mode in which advocates offer evidence and argument to a neutral third party to obtain a decision in their favor. Virtually all public managers settle disputes, some concerning differences the agency has with its stakeholders and some regarding internal differences with or between agency members.

Formal administrative adjudication results from law (statute, regulation, or court order) that requires or permits its use. It involves the services of specialized administrators called administrative law judges (ALJs) or hearing examiners. Disputes in these forums are usually presented as discrete, with one or a few narrowly defined issues, two or a very small number of parties, and a need to find facts already in existence but disputed. Sometimes, the decisions have far-ranging policy implications (for example, in order to settle a dispute, a critical provision in a collective bargaining agreement has to be interpreted).

Federal and state administrative procedure acts and judicial opinions largely define the way in which these officials conduct their hearing tasks. They are not judges and they are not presiding over trials, in the legal sense; thus they are not committed to running their hearings like trials, with all that might entail for the use of rules of evidence and other legal profession methods. Despite this freedom, there is considerable difference of opinion among ALJs and hearing examiners as to whether they should strive to conduct their hearings as though they were trials. The name change from "hearing examiner" to "administrative law judge" brought about by their professional organization lobbying efforts in federal and many state governments gives evidence that most do. Some, clearly a minority, prefer to think of themselves as specialized administrators conducting more informal hearings. The danger is that they too may closely identify with the judicial role, thus creating additional pressures for inefficient and inappropriate judicialization practices.

Informal adjudication is far more common, normally exercised by ordinary managers acting to implement public policy or to resolve conflicts in the workplace. In such disputes, procedures are rarely set down and issues can be tangled and ill-defined. Often, the matter presents itself in a way that does not suggest a dispute, as when an employee complains about but seems to accept a ruling (for example, that travel time connected with medical consultation cannot be taken as sick leave). In such circumstances, the just adjudicator must be able to discern whether the complainant feels an injustice has occurred and to locate the points of difference. Where the presence of dispute is clear, a climate and procedures should be established to encourage persons who feel unjustly treated to air their real or alleged grievances.

A wide range of hearing settings exists between formal, APA-style, or arbitration hearings on one end and informal hearings on the other. Difficult to generalize, these hearings are usually conducted on the basis of internal written policies by an administrator or staff employee.

In adjudicating any dispute, the just adjudicator should possess knowledge of the constitutional requirements of due process. In an informal dispute, this may consist of nothing more than telling the disputant about a proposed action, showing him the evidence upon which it is based, and allowing him the opportunity to respond (*Goss v. Lopez*, 1975). Also, the just adjudicator should respect the dignity and special circumstances of the parties to the dispute. Finally, the just administrator should be attuned to the political position of stakeholders, how they stand with reference to policies the agency is administering, and their relationship to others not directly involved in the dispute but likely to be affected by the decision.

Policymaker. When the public administrator exercises discretionary authority delegated by political superiors, she may be creating policy, interpreting policy, or making an implementation decision. In the policy-creating role, the administrator takes on a social justice dimension because she is engaging in an *initial* allocational judgment involving the distribution of social benefits and burdens. In the second instance, a broad, prior political guideline operates, and the administrator interprets the guideline in such a way as to give it flesh and meaning. In both lawmaking and interpretive roles, the decision is often the outcome of a well-regulated process, as in rulemaking under Section 553 of the APA. But it is also frequently made simply by order of an administrative officer acting with or without the advice of staff. Or it may be brought about by a process entailing consultation with interested stakeholders and consensus building or compromise. The third type of discretionary exercise, implementation, is simply that of choosing among alternative means in order to reach a policy judgment already made, although the choice of means can influence and shape policy.

What does justice require of the public administrator acting in the role of policymaker? The just policymaker must

1. Be willing and able to discover legislative intent or other evidence of a general political consensus from which to draw authority to act
2. Bring to bear on the decision relevant technical expertise
3. Use democratic techniques to resolve conflict, which involves promoting participation of the affected stakeholders, surfacing differing positions and values to be aired, and seeking consensus

Manager. The quintessential role in public administration is the job of managing public programs. It may not be immediately obvious, but the traditional managerial functions of planning, budgeting, staffing, directing, organizing, coordinating and evaluating contain a rich trove of justice elements, related to both outcome and procedure.

The discretionary choices managers make relative to implementation determine to a considerable degree the success of public programs, which, ultimately, translates to how much of the promised public policy is delivered to the people. Justice simply requires that they learn to do their jobs well, that they learn and apply effective and accepted managerial techniques. This certainly includes demanding good performance from subordinates and being able to use discipline if that is required for achieving performance. Hiring, promotion, overtime assignment, and separation decisions should be based on merit standards, except as these may be overridden by general policy considerations such as affirmative action or veterans preference.

Managers are the "shock troops" for the fallout of disillusionment, unhappiness, and burdens experienced by both citizens and employees as program activities spin themselves out. To facilitate program implementation, managers must anticipate and work out the inevitable conflicts that arise as the result of the clash of program goals and the interests of citizens and groups who resist or are adversely affected by the program's operation. They must maintain grievance procedures promoting the informal, quick, and fair resolution of employee grievances.

Managers, if they are to motivate their people toward accomplishing public policy goals, must become expert at establishing the conditions, routines, and procedures for orderly and fair informal dispute resolution. Turning to agency legal counsel for answers or deflecting disputants to specialized adjudication tribunals may be necessary or appropriate in particular cases, when litigation threatens or constitutional rights are involved. But formal process is a high-cost remedy that may compromise program goals, because it translates to the consuming of scarce resources, time, and program energies. This presents the dilemma of balancing rights protection against organizational effectiveness and efficiency.

The solution to the dilemma lies in the agency being able, primarily at the level of the program manager, to resolve disputes informally. The just manager must have the ability to sense potential and emerging disputes and take action to head them off. This entails knowing the interests of both clients and employees and being able to relate program activities to them. The manager must give special attention to the talents and needs of employees for career development and for assuming responsibility and to potential discrimination factors in the composition of the workforce, such as race, ethnicity, gender, and AIDS. Such attention should help the manager to be aware of felt injustices.

When disputes survive preventive action and become full blown, the just manager must employ conflict management skills in a way consistent with the principles of due process. The personal attributes of optimism and a sense of fairness seem essential to the task.

Supervisor of Professionals. Public administrators, such as the heads of staff units composed primarily of engineers, biologists, social workers, and other professionals, play a special role. They are usually themselves members of the same professions that their subordinates belong to and are able to understand the core of professional knowledge used by their subordinates. They are therefore in a position to translate that expertise and make it usable to the larger organization in the pursuit of its objectives.

Mosher (1982) commented upon the tendency of professionals to divide their loyalties between their organization and their profession. Such persons, he observes, fall prey to narrowness of vision engendered by their education and professional training and the norms of their professional associations. An engineer working in a state highway department may be more interested in the internal design features of a transportation project than its utility or environmental or esthetic impact on the community, ends that may be clearly sought in public policy. The professional supervisor's job is to crosswalk between the narrower professional view and the broader public interest.

What does justice require of the professional supervisor? As an individual who crosswalks between the agency leadership and the professional core group upon whom the leadership must rely, the professional supervisor has a special obligation to keep in mind agency objectives and to translate them into terms that his employees can understand. A great deal of attention to the professional sensibilities of subordinates is required, lest the latter are made to feel deprived of their professional status and the discretionary latitude that can be expected to flow from it.

Advocate. Public administrators are frequently called upon to represent their units and programs within the agency, before legislatures, to political executives, and to the public at large. A common problem related to advocacy in organizations is "suboptimization," or the tendency to put the goals and interests of the subunit ahead of those of the parent organization (Merton, 1949). There is a difference between suboptimization and the kind of active promotion of a unit or program that promotes all of the policy goals of the agency.

Administrative justice requires that the advocate convey information about her unit's performance accurately and insist that other units and programs do the same. If suboptimization is to be dealt with, and the organization and the public are to be well served, scrupulous care should be given that organizational leadership has a clear picture of what is going on in its various units and that every unit is playing by the rules.

The advocate walks a fine line in balancing the unit's needs with larger organizational needs. Justice requires that the unit's interests be forcefully stated and the interests of its members promoted, representing the legitimate expectations of those represented. On the other hand, these worthy ends should not be allowed to obscure the vision of organizational leadership. This is one of those moral ambiguities that Bailey would have appreciated: An advocate should be aggressive and persuasive but not so aggressive and persuasive that he or she interferes with the ability of the larger organization to properly assess its strengths and weaknesses and bring these to bear on its decisions. If the advocate portrays her unit or program as more capable or successful than it truly is, she contributes to the risk of creating a misallocation of public resources. On the other hand, if other units are unfairly promoting themselves out of proportion to their worth, playing the "good citizen" will most likely cause unfair proportional harm to her unit.

There is also a special obligation on the part of the just advocate to understand the relationship of the unit's goals to the broader public policy objectives and to the legitimate clients of the organization. It is possible that a unit's mission is on course so far as the policy is concerned but that the agency has strayed. It is then the just advocate's duty to point up the greater fidelity of the unit to the overall policy goal or to the client, a course of action that is likely to require courage.

Public Role Model. Public administrators influence public perceptions of their agencies and of government generally through their behavior. In this role, which may not be so much a role as it is the effect of accumulated perceptions, the way in which the administrator's behavior is perceived may be more crucial than what is actually done. Like Caesar's wife, the administrator should be above suspicion. If the administrator is seen as fair and reasonable or as unfair and unreasonable, it is fair to say that his agency or program will be seen accordingly. Accumulated perceptions of a variety of government actors will build up to color the views of citizens relative to the government generally.

The just administrator must recognize that the public judges behavior, whether related to official or personal life, in relation to his official role and to the reputation of the agency. For example, an ethnic joke by an agency official in the course of a speech may be taken by an audience to mean that both the administrator and the agency make decisions in part on the basis of ethnicity. Administrators should be seeking to create images of themselves, their programs, and their agencies that bespeak the values of participation, responsiveness, equal access, regarding the public service as a trust, and above all even-handed fairness.

Is an injustice perpetrated if the administrator succeeds in building an image that is untrue and better than the reality? This type of deception is a kind of injustice, discussed in the following chapter, that stems from the agency's lying to the public about what it is doing or what it has accomplished. Management at the Rocky Flats plutonium weapons plant near Denver for years cultivated the image that it was directing a group of scientists in closely monitoring levels of radiation contamination, playing the role of good citizens vitally interested in the welfare of the community. These projections were false and known to be so by those who made them at the time they were made. James Watkins, secretary of energy, concluded that such an image interferes with the long-term effectiveness of the agency and that openness and candor are essential if the agency is to win back the public respect needed to do its job (Easterbrook, 1990). As we have argued consistently throughout this book, openness is essential to administrative justice.

Consumer of Goods and Services. Administrators often purchase goods and services and lead units that do this task. Goods and services are normally supplied by private businesses and less frequently by other government units. Rules of competitive bidding and quality control apply to this process and are seen by the general public and political superiors as essential to prevent fraud and waste. Conflict of interest laws must be scrupulously observed. These requirements, taken together, create an unsettling climate in which procurement officers are subject to a variety of strict sanctions. Adding to the tension is the fact that the law's concern reaches beyond the workplace into the personal life of the procurement official. Property owned and persons with whom business is transacted are proper subjects for inquiry.

Although use of the efficiency standard of lowest cost is the usual method for selecting winning contract bids, other distributive justice standards are frequently used. Spreading the business around to heighten the perception of fairness, selecting on the basis of merit factors, and awarding a set percentage of contracts to minority businesses are distributive justice criteria that can also be defended.

Justice requires that the administrator with procurement responsibilities be aware of even remote possibilities of conflict of interest and, when they appear, shift decision responsibility to others who are free of conflict. The role of being a manager of a procurement unit entails special considerations. The manager must take care to provide training to procurement specialists so they can recognize potential conflicts of interest and be able to raise the issues. Also, in case of challenge, guidelines must be fashioned to take into account standards other than efficiency and to justify decisions based upon them.

The Administrator's Responsibility to Build
the Just Organization

Yet more is required of the administrator who would be just than to internalize the justice elements associated with the various general and special roles she may fill. To build the just organization, public administration practitioners and academicians having values consistent with those of justice must act as change agents to bring about the conditions that allow movement toward a just organizational culture.

It is a mistake to think that changes in this direction will be forced from outside the organization through law change or codes of professional ethics. Hierarchy and top-down authority, although somewhat weakened by professionalism and unionization in the past generation, are still the most powerful influences upon organizational behavior. What is needed is the conversion of public administration *leadership* in all of its various roles to habits and attitudes consistent with the criteria of just administrative decisions.

Conversion of public administration leadership to the cause of justice can only occur if, as Stephen Bailey tells us, noble ideas are combined with a persuasive appeal to self-interest. Does administrative justice contain this elegant pragmatism? It is just possible that it does. To the extent that the bureaucracy continues to be threatened by declining prestige, shrinking revenues, and the outflow of talented people, the instinct to survive may fuel the self-interest of public servants in sound, mainstream normative theory. Short of such a continuing crisis, hopes for conversion will have to rest upon other factors: the continued pressure of the courts on administration for administrative reform, awakening interest of public service professional and civic organizations in ethics, and the obvious appeal of justice as a decision framework for making superior and admirable decisions.

7

UNDERSTANDING
AND RESPONDING
TO INJUSTICE

Thus far this book has concentrated upon a model of administrative *justice*. For the most part, the model focuses on what happens, or should happen, after basic policy directions have been set through constitutional-political processes. It recognizes the discretionary power of the bureaucracy to make policy interstitially and, once policy is made, it assumes the validity of the policies and rules of the regime, both political and bureaucratic, with one important exception. The exception is that when a rule or a policy is in conflict with the principle intended by the lawmaker, the administrative justice model directs that a just decision must favor the principle over the rule. Reduced to its essentials, the model is primarily concerned with making sure that persons and groups in society get what is due to them under the law as legitimate lawmakers intended and that they are treated fairly in the process.

We have generally avoided dealing with broader questions of social justice, that is, the policies the lawmakers should have adopted in the first place. In the pluralistic, money- and image-driven environment that defines American politics, imperfect results can be expected. Political contexts favor those who possess financial resources, knowledge, and superior organization over those who lack these attributes. The resulting public policy product tends to reflect this imbalance and, to an important degree, to produce injustices within government. Under these circumstances, the administrator's mission must include the protection of any unfair advantage that has already been achieved.

What, if anything, can or ought to be done by the bureaucracy to respond to social injustice? It seems clear that the injustice endemic in our society and in our basic laws can only partially be ameliorated through administrative justice. If administrators go too far in the direction of undoing what seem to them unjust laws, they will undermine their legitimacy and threaten the integrity of the democratic process. Yet few among us would take the position that the administrator must stand idly by. There ought to be a middle position to command, one that protects the integrity of the law while seeking greater justice for those who feel they have been mistreated in the broader realm of social justice.

The purpose of this chapter is to further the search for this middle position, to stake out the boundaries within which it may be found. We take the approach that public administrators need to be aware of how government creates injustice, both by themselves in the performance of their various roles and by those in political positions external to the agencies. Bureaucrats need to be sensitized to and respond to the *sense of injustice* that permeates the thinking and motivates the behavior of so many of the citizens, persons, and groups with whom they are in constant interaction.

The Sense of Injustice

Injustice precedes justice just as surely as hunger precedes nourishment. Strong emotions arise in those who have the sense that they have been treated unjustly. Next to the need to survive, it is perhaps the most intense of all human emotions. According to Carl Friedrich, "It is a remarkable fact that men's feelings are more sharply aroused by an act of injustice than by one of justice. Whatever may be the psychological reasons for this fact—and they are many—the existential ground on which it rests is the threat to the beliefs and values cherished by a person and the consequent anxiety induced in him. An unjust act causes a man anguish because it not only challenges a particular belief and value, but, owing to the interrelation of such beliefs and values, it challenges the community as a system of shared values and beliefs" (1963, p. 30).

The sense of injustice is the special kind of anger that is felt when promises are not delivered and when people feel they have been deprived by the act of another of something due them. It is based upon "our natural ability to feel deprived, humiliated, and offended when our expectations as human beings are not met" (Shklar, 1990, p. 87). The sense of injustice is compounded when it is witnessed by a third person and the latter does nothing to prevent it. When a government official witnesses an injustice being done to a citizen but does nothing, a double injustice is perpetrated—a second deprivation occurs because the citizen has an expectation violated that government will intercede on her behalf.

In political terms, the citizen's grievance occupies "the core of the modern democratic political sensibility" (Shklar, 1990, pp. 83–84). Whether the injustice claimed is truly an injustice (as opposed to a misfortune) or whether the claim is one that can be recognized and acted upon under the law, the democratic ethic requires that the victim be heard. The victim's voice "is the privileged voice" because without her voice it is impossible to decide whether an injustice has been done (Shklar, 1990, p. 90). Democracy does not put an end to injustice; it lends dignity to individual voice and thereby serves to keep political passions within bounds.

At its heart, the sense of injustice is the psychological phenomenon of feeling deprived of something we believe is rightfully due us. Sometimes that which is denied is well defined and clear and legally due us (for example, the right to receive public assistance if eligibility requirements are met); sometimes it is ill defined and not established as a legal right (not being asked our opinion when our position or expertise suggests that we be consulted). However defined, these felt deprivations are what we mean when we speak of a sense of injustice.

Government Injustice

Citizen expectations of government interventions on their behalf keep escalating. Through much of human history, "the gods" or cruel fortune or foreign invaders were most frequently identified as the agents of victimization. In the modern, technologically developed world in which all seems possible, government and its agents have increasingly been seen as the culprits. Even "acts of God" may be attributed to government misconduct, as when rising water destroys a home in a flood plain and the homeowner had no prior notice from the bank that the home was in a precarious area. The responsible government agency "should have done something" and gotten the word out so as to have allowed the victim to avoid purchasing the house.

Injustice enters into the decision process of public organizations in many ways, some of which are dimly perceived. To the layperson, the sources of unjust decisions, actions, or inactions by government agencies may appear to be uncomplicated and straightforward. "Bureaucratic bungling," "red tape," "insensitivity," "laziness," "favoritism," "incompetence," and "prejudice" are widely used reasons in the media and in ordinary parlance to explain why "things go wrong."

Occasionally, these formulations of the causes of injustice are correct. More often, they are not. We have no idea of the frequency with which injustice occurs as the result of the bad habits or inadequacies of agency officials, but in the pages that follow it should become obvious that injustice springs from a variety of causes. Public administrators can exercise little or no control over many of them, and some they can influence only with the expenditure of great effort.

Many injustices attributed to the bureaucracy actually originate in the political and social environment that surrounds public organizations rather than in the agencies themselves. Others flow from the inherent nature of policy change, or from a lack of resources preventing administrators from doing the job they know how to do. And, of course, many injustices do arise from the workings of public organizations and from the behaviors, attitudes, and decisions of their members. The next section clarifies and explains the primary sources and types of administrative injustice.

Categories of Administrative Injustice

The source of the injustice that occurs in administrative agencies may be external, rising in the broader social and political environment, or it may be internal, rooted in the agencies' attitudes, routines, or practices. Further, the injustice may have its source in an act or omission of a single actor (or small group), or it may be the result of a system of relationships, rules, and practices. It is useful to be aware of these various possible sources to determine where accountability for injustice lies and to formulate strategy to alleviate or remove them.

The categories of the sources of injustice that follow are created through the interaction of two variables: (1) point of origin (the original source within or outside the agency) and (2) attribution to an individual or to "the system." The first is chosen because it seems important to distinguish between the responsibility of public administration and that of other political system actors for injustice. This should mitigate the unfortunate but popular practice of attributing the sins of the larger political and social worlds to the bureaucracy. The latter variable is chosen because knowing whether the injustice results from individual action or a "system" problem helps to fix accountability as well as to suggest the measures to be taken to right the injustice. If an injustice can be determined to be the result of the act of an individual or a small group of individuals, remediation might proceed in the form of public exposure, punishment, training, or some combination of these. If, on the other hand, an injustice can be demonstrated to be the result of the workings of "many hands" (too many actors are involved to permit the attachment of accountability to one or a few), or "no hands" (the decision seems to be impelled by the procedures or rules and accountability cannot be attached to anyone or even a group), correction would proceed on some other basis (such as organizational redesign or the revamping of information, communications, or decision processes).

Thinking simultaneously about these two distinctions leads to the conceptualization presented in the matrix shown in Figure 7.1. In the upper left-hand cell (external source and individual causation) are found injustices not under the control of public organizations, which are initially caused by individuals outside the organization (Type I injustices). Such persons are likely to be legislators or elected executives or their staffs who act with volition. In Cell II (external source and system causation) reside injustices that result initially from sources outside of the agency, attributable to general conditions rather than the will of some particular actor or group. These Type II injustices include a lack of resources to adequately fund agency action or excessive policy complexity that precludes effective action.

Figure 7.1. Types of Administrative Injustice and Examples of Each.

CAUSATIVE AGENT

		INDIVIDUAL	SYSTEM
S O U R C E	**E X T E R N A L**	**I** • Unjust laws • Undue pressure from elected officials	**II** • Underfunding • Rapid policy change
	I N T E R N A L	**III** • Unethical acts of administrators • Irrational acts of administrators	**IV** • Workflow problems • Suboptimization

Although public administration may have no responsibility for the *creation* of Type I or Type II injustices, it may well have a responsibility for doing something about their *correction* (Davis, 1969; Burke, 1986; Shklar, 1990). If bureaucrats know about a preventable injustice but stand idly by, they compound the injustice through their inaction. "The attitude is that as long as the injustice is caused by the statute, the administrator has no reason for concern. One major responsibility of every agency . . . is to watch for deficiencies in the legislation it administers, and to make systematic recommendations for changes. . . . Administrators must share the responsibility for producing legislation that is sound, workable, and just. . . ." (Davis, 1969, p. 53).

Public administrators are proactive agents in the political system. Because of their special knowledge and expertise in particular policy areas, and because they take an oath to serve the constitution and the people, they play a necessary role in the remediation of "bad policy."

The cells labeled III and IV (internal source and individual causation, and internal source and system causation, respectively) contain those injustices most clearly within public administration's control and responsibility. Type III injustices tend to be the result of illegal, immoral, or at least wrongheaded actions, inactions, or attitudes of public administrators. Type IV injustices relate to systemic problems within agencies or programs that interfere with delivering that which is due to people. These clearly include all the typical problems of organizing and managing that public administrators face daily: problems relating to how to collect, organize, retrieve, and use information; how to communicate and encourage people to work together; and how to acquire and effectively use people with essential expertise and special knowledge.

Any of the injustices in any of the four cells of the matrix may affect either of two broad classes: (1) the general public, interest groups, or other public organizations and (2) persons and groups within the agency, including its employees, managers, and others (such as contractors or legislative staff) who are integrally associated with the agency and its decision-making apparatus.

Type I Injustices

The sources of injustice that are external to administrative agencies and rooted in individual or small group actions or inactions are of many sorts, including, but not limited to, the following cases.

Political pressure to demonstrate the success of a policy may cause neglect of the policy principle. An example was the deplorable practice of taking body counts by the agents of intelligence and military units during the Vietnam fighting to bolster White House claims that the war was being waged successfully. Such pressure makes it more likely to lose sight of real purposes, to make false estimates of effectiveness, and to place emphasis on false proxies of goal achievement. In the case of Vietnam, the administration of both military and diplomatic units allowed itself to be distracted from its primary policy purpose, which was to keep South Vietnam out of the hands of the Communist North.

Political leaders may press the agency to pursue goals in ways other than those envisaged in the law. The Challenger shuttle disaster may well be an example of this phenomenon. Presidential pressures to demonstrate the program's commercial viability are alleged to have overridden the pleas of the government subcontractor's engineers that the policy goal of safety was being ignored (Cooper, 1987).

Political leaders may appoint the type of top agency officials that they calculate are likely to bring about the policy's failure. The leaders select officials who do not share an enthusiasm for the program objectives or who are incompetent or lack energy or imagination. This charge was frequently heard at the beginning of President Reagan's first term regarding his initial appointments (and delay in appointing anyone) to regulatory agencies, the missions of which Mr. Reagan had attacked when he was a candidate.

Type II Injustices

Instances in which injustices are caused by external forces or conditions, not associated with individuals, are common. They arise in the following sets of circumstances.

1. Resources become scarce or are not adequate to begin with. Programs are stretched beyond their effective limits. As a result, some beneficiaries designated by law are neglected, essential personnel are not hired, economies are sought in agency budgets irrespective of their effects upon goal achievement, and so forth.

2. New interests and rights are recognized. Resources and attention are shifted away from old interests that were once favored to accommodate new ones. Important policy changes alter the mix of winners and losers. For example, the New York State Human Rights Commission reallocated its staff to concentrate more attention on AIDS discrimination, thus reducing the attention given to race, sex, and other types of illegal discrimination. Another common but older example is that of persons being given less consideration in hiring or promotion because of the adoption of affirmative action policies. Shklar reasons: "Almost every new law, however benign, displaces someone's expectations and plans and arouses their sense of injustice, often violently. That is why in constitutional governments laws are passed slowly and in public, so that individuals can adjust their plans to new legal conditions. Every social change, every new law, every forced alteration of public rules is unjust to someone. The more drastic and sudden the change, the greater the grievances" (1990, p. 120).

3. The pace of change is very rapid. The bureaucracy is not programmed to deal with the new types of decision routines that rapid, externally generated policy change demand. The effort required to understand the dynamics of new situations and to develop decision routines to cope with them is great. Breakdowns occur. This is not a problem of internal inefficiency so much as a problem flowing from the inability

of bureaucratic organizations to respond quickly to change imposed upon them. Bureaucracies can deal well with exceptions to a general policy or pattern with which it is familiar.

Responsibility for Correcting Type I and Type II Injustices. When an agency becomes convinced that a policy external lawmakers have handed it is unfair or unworkable, it has an obligation to act. Its obligation to act is inherent in the special knowledge and expertise of its technical and professional staff and in the oath of office taken by its administrative leaders to "faithfully execute the law."

Depending upon its view of its role and responsibility and its political leverage, the agency can choose among various courses of action. It can (1) use whatever discretionary powers it has to set policy on the right course, for example, broad rulemaking authority; (2) attempt to influence external lawmakers to change the law; (3) report back to the lawmaker that the policy is not working or is working to create injustice, and its opinion as to why; or (4) do a combination of these things. Of course, the agency is duty bound to attempt to implement the original policy in good faith, but if it becomes convinced of the policy's unworkability, its continued efforts along that line would simply be wasteful of resources. Under the first option, it can use its delegated and inherent authority to interpret the law's provisions to make the policy workable or fair in line with the lawmaker's intent, even if the effect of the reinterpretation is to cause it to deviate from some rules contained in the policy. If the agency lacks discretionary authority or the will to exercise it, administrators might still elect to act as advocates or simply as reporters before policymaking bodies.

Administrative injustice lies in the unwillingness of the agency to do anything, in the fact that it remains passive under circumstances where it has the expertise, special knowledge, and opportunity to create pressure to effect a more likely path to policy achievement.

Type III Injustices

These are situations that most closely conform to popular notions about the sources of injustice in administrative settings. In this category are situations where organizational agents are acting (or not acting) in ways that are creating injustices. Agency officials are (1) violating the law or policy they are obligated to implement, (2) intentionally misrepresenting facts to reduce public scrutiny or criticism, (3) managing the policy in a way intended to frustrate the law's purpose, (4) engaging in exploitation or discrimination against employees, and (5) committing misdeeds (theft, corruption, and so on) or condoning the misdeeds of others.

Policy Violations. Imagine the rather common situation in which the agency decision maker is, for whatever purpose, at odds with policy that enjoys the status of law and acts to deny or redirect benefits or block sanctions contemplated by the law. If we assume that there is no lack of clarity about what the law states or means, the situation is that the administrative decision maker has chosen to act in defiance of that law he or she is obligated by law or oath to enforce. Funds set aside for executing the law are either wasted, reallocated, or never spent, with the result that those who were intended by the lawmakers to receive the benefit of the policy are deprived of that which is due them.

The Iran-Contra hearings in 1987 and the subsequent trials of Lieutenant Colonel Oliver North and Admiral John Poindexter of the National Security Agency (NSA) afford a good example of intentional subversion of law. Poindexter, the NSA chief, his assistant North, and others arranged arms sales to Iran in return for the release of hostages held in Lebanon. They then diverted funds from the sales to the military support of Nicaraguan "Contra" rebels at the very time that Congress had made it illegal to give other than humanitarian, nonmilitary aid to the Contras. North and Poindexter, although not conceding that the law applied to the NSA, were openly hostile to the law and to Congress playing a role in Central American foreign policy. Their actions negated laws that had been authoritatively established as the result of a constitutional and democratic process.

Other illustrations can be drawn from very different settings. A California court recently found that the University of California violated a frequently reaffirmed federal act that provides federal money for land-grant university agricultural stations to conduct research intended to preserve small family farms. With this grant money, the university helped developed a tomato harvester that transformed the industry in California, cutting jobs from 50,000 in 1964 to less than 18,000 in 1970 and the number of tomato growers from 4,000 in 1963 to 597 in 1973. The plaintiff, California Action Network, alleged that "not a penny was spent to study the implications of mechanization on jobs, on farm size, on prices, on the environment." The judge found that the university had violated the policy and ordered it to develop a detailed plan for complying with the act (Sinclair, 1987).

Misrepresentation of Fact. Official lying, misleading by giving half-truths, and failure to correct misinformation the agency knows the public to have are not uncommon. In an old but poignant example, the officer in charge of radiological safety of the Pacific Ocean atomic testing program wrote a memo in 1946 to U.S. Army General Groves about the insidious danger of radioactive fallout. Minute amounts of fallout particles would enter the human body, the officer wrote, and would lead eventually to progressive anemia and death. He concluded: "I believe a frank statement of this sort should be made now to professional and intelligent lay groups as part of the general discussion on the effect of the bomb as a whole . . ." (Ball, 1986, p. 204). The Atomic Energy Commission deliberately chose not to share his professional and official opinion and the facts upon which it was based, instead choosing to equate radioactive fallout with dental X-rays.

Frustration of the Law. Administrators also may seek to nullify or emasculate the effect of the law through actions short of direct violation or misrepresentation of fact. Such action may be thought of as frustrating rather than violating the law. Strategies vary, but all share the feature that the policy is intentionally made more difficult to implement. An administrator may attempt to undermine the policy's implementation by (1) confusing the law's application by unduly complicating it, (2) staffing programs with people who are known to be hostile to them, (3) foot-dragging, (4) deliberate underfunding, (5) requiring largely duplicative checks and reviews before decisions can take effect, (6) delaying error correction through cumbersome procedural rules, or (7) confining the effect of error correction to single cases rather than to the policy as a whole. This list is not exhaustive, and a great deal of creativity has been exercised in frustrating the achievement of policy objectives.

The United Steelworkers of America sought contempt citations against the federal budget director and an assistant secretary of labor in a federal court on the ground that they were blocking the issuance by the Occupational Safety and Health Administration (OSHA) of court-ordered warnings to 18 million workers about the dangers of toxic chemicals. The court had ordered OSHA to issue regulations for the labeling of hazardous chemicals in 3.5 million workplaces by August 1987. The department was to levy fines of up to $10,000 each against firms not posting appropriate warnings in workplaces where the rules required them. The Office of Management and Budget (OMB) delayed carrying out the order, arguing that some of the regulation's provisions were contrary to the Paperwork Reduction Act ("Contempt Citations . . . ," 1988). This case may be seen as an attempt to justify noncompliance with one law by way of pointing to the arguably inconsistent requirements of another law.

A good example of using procedure to delay or prevent action was the Veterans Administration's handling of claims filed by veterans who were exposed to the chemical "agent orange" in Vietnam. The agency routinely denied these claims while at the same time failing to make available to claimants a clear statement of the criteria it was using (if indeed it used any) to decide upon the merits of the claims.

David Schmeltzer, compliance division chief of the Consumer Product Safety Commission since 1977, was removed from his position in 1987 to work on a field study. His attorney charged that Schmeltzer had been exiled from his post because he dissented publicly from positions taken by commission chairman Terrence M. Scanlon, who favored working with industry to prevent product dangers and resolve safety issues. Consumer groups charged that Scanlon paralyzed the agency with staff transfers and blocked action to ban dangerous products. Republican Senator Alfonse D'Amato (New York) was quoted as saying Scanlon was transfixed by "some crazy ideology that says we never interfere with the marketplace," an attitude that D'Amato, himself a self-proclaimed conservative, said would "destroy the enforcement effort, deliberately" (Specter, 1987).

Whatever distributive justice standard agency decision makers use to bring about the distribution of public goods, they may apply it in unequal, uninformed, irrational, or arbitrary ways. The causes vary. For example, the decision maker may have a bias rooted in self-interest, may not have sought the information needed to make a fair decision, or may be excessively influenced by one of the participants in the decision process.

Exploitation and Discrimination. A public manager may take intentional or unintentional advantage of a citizen or an employee for personal or organizational gain. The unjust decision may take the form of an unjustified benefit being given to an employee, such as a promotion awarded on the basis of friendship or yielding to sexual demands. The injustice is two-fold: first, the abuse—mental, physical, or economic—of one person by another as a function of the manager's position; second, a misallocation of public resources by virtue of a less efficient use of human resources. Sexual harassment, nepotism, and racial discrimination are obvious examples of exploitative behavior. Using persons as test subjects without their having full knowledge of potential consequences may also fall within this category.

Not so obvious are decisions that discriminate among citizens or employees on the basis of factors having no legitimate legal or goal-serving function. Included are differing treatment based on life-style (sexual preference, dress, and manner of speech), physical appearance (obesity, lack of attractiveness), physical condition (handicap, disease, pregnancy), and status prior to employment (residency, alien status, conviction for crime). Retaliation against an employee for exercising constitutional, statutory, or organizational (for example, grievance) rights is a particularly virulent form of discrimination because it discourages the bringing to light and possible correction of many instances of injustice.

Managers, as much through neglect as by design, will sometimes deny employees certain job-related rights or take away job responsibilities. In doing so, managers may violate the law or act immorally. The decision takes the form of denying to the citizen or employee some right or expectation that is rightfully theirs, or imposing some burden that is not. Decisions on hiring and promotion, separations, work assignments, and other job-related matters (award of overtime, training, and so on) often fall into this category.

As an illustration, a female charged that the District of Columbia police department performed pregnancy tests on prospective employees. To do so, it allegedly used urine samples of female job applicants that had been taken supposedly to test for drug usage. The department's personnel officer defended the practice, arguing that the agency does not discriminate but would only defer hiring until after the pregnancy period (Black, 1987). If true, the employer was acting illegally in denying prospective employees a constitutional right of privacy and in unfairly discriminating in the hiring process. There is the potential danger that the employer could also use such samples to search for diseases such as AIDS and diabetes and medicines used in psychiatric care or in conjunction with certain physical disorders.

The Iran-Contra committee's final report criticized the Pentagon for failing to review or remove the security clearances of Oliver North, for shredding documents needed in the

Department of Justice's criminal investigation, and of John Poindexter, for ripping up a highly sensitive presidential intelligence authorization. Meanwhile, Fawn Hall, North's former secretary, who participated in the shredding but who also cooperated in the investigation, had her security clearance reviewed and her access to classified material stopped (Pincus, 1987). Differential treatment is clearly evident.

Other common examples include a manager's assigning an employee to work in a job above his own job class without additional pay; hiring on the basis of friendship, whim, self-protection, or other subjective grounds not related to organizational needs; and assigning overtime work consistently to one or a few among a group of qualified persons.

Misdeeds. Committing or condoning the commission of illegal or wrong acts by others, including employees and agency clients, is the last and perhaps most frequent instance of internally generated injustices springing from volitional conduct. These range from petty wrongs such as taking home office supplies and making personal long-distance telephone calls on the job to more egregious acts such as accepting bribes, stealing large sums of money, committing sexual offenses, or perjuring oneself on a job application or benefit eligibility form. All such acts allocate resources away from the implementation of public policy and thus are injustices committed against the public. However, it is the knowledge by agency officials of a misdeed or a pattern of misdeeds, and subsequent inaction through condoning or neglect, that converts the injustice into administrative injustice.

It is at least arguable that even if agency officials do not know of such misdeeds, their failure to put in place a system for seeking them out and acting upon them when discovered also constitutes administrative injustice. A schoolteacher was convicted of child molestation in an incident at a public school in the 1960s. Years later, he was hired to a teaching position in a second state, fraudulently omitting the fact of his conviction from his application. He was convicted a second time for a similar crime while employed in the second position. Again, years later, he applied for and was hired to a teaching position in yet a third state! (CBS News, 1987). The lack of effort made by school personnel officials to run a simple background check, not the criminal act by the teacher, is the root of this possible Type III injustice.

Type IV Injustices

The fourth cell of the matrix presents the case where problems caused by internal system design faults and organizational inefficiencies lead to injustice. Program implementation is impeded, with resulting deprivation for individual citizens and groups. In this scenario, some operational problem is interfering with the implementation of policy that is within the agency's power to eliminate or alleviate.

The basic problem may be one of organizational structure; planning, staffing, operating, or decision procedures; or patterns of organizational behavior. The root causes are varied and numerous, such as outmoded organizational rules and routines, shortages in professional and skilled staff, information gaps and communication failures, or simple human error. No less than the whole of the notion of "good management" is potentially involved.

Most of these problems are described and addressed in Chapter Five, which concerns obstacles to institutionalizing justice in public organizations. However, a few examples of the injustices flowing from these systemic problems are appropriate to illustrate this category of injustices.

A young woman, orphaned and illiterate, was committed to a state mental hospital by her brother after suffering an epileptic seizure, and she stayed for fifty-eight years. A psychiatrist interviewed her upon her admission, and her record showed an original diagnosis of "psychosis, equivalent of epilepsy." *The entire medical record for the first twelve years of confinement occupied less than one page.* A hospital worker said the patient had and still has a wonderful mind. Mental health officials now say she never should have been there and that such an incident could not now occur under the state's procedural guidelines (Evans, 1987).

Claus Barbie, "the butcher of Leon" and a Nazi war criminal, was employed by the U.S. Army immediately after World War II under an assumed identity. He was valued for his intellect and his knowledge of Soviet intelligence matters. He was known to have been a Nazi but it was not known (at least, to most of those he worked with) that he had been an SS officer. Failure of his unit to communicate with another army unit that gathered information on and tracked war criminals permitted Barbie to be retained until French investigators exploded his cover and forced Barbie to flee to South America (with support from the U.S. Army and the Vatican). Intelligence units tend to operate in secrecy, and it was probable that his employing unit either did not know or did not want to know his background in view of his services; no rule or procedure was in effect that would force that knowledge to emerge. The pieces of information that could have exposed Barbie existed among U.S. Army and French intelligence units but were never brought together. Thus it was that the incredible injustice of protecting a murderous war criminal was perpetrated (U.S. Department of Justice, 1983).

Error Correction. It is inevitable that an organization will make mistakes that will have negative consequences for people. This fact, in and of itself, does not have to lead to an injustice. But the lack of an effective error correction system is a system deficiency that almost certainly will lead to injustice. In a democratic society, appeal and complaint routes should be provided by and within public organizations for citizens, external organizations, or agency employees to seek an independent review of virtually all decisions they believe are unjust.

It is critical that independent review be provided within public organizations. Part of the reason for this is that practical difficulties exist that hinder access to each of the political branches for review. Appeals to the courts are severely limited by the latter's own restrictive rules for the review of cases. Complaints about administrative action made to legislators may be treated with less than adequate care. Worse, many legislators simply call on the allegedly culpable agency to supply the answers, and these are passed on the complainant. Executive branch persons, in a hierarchical relationship to most agencies, have a predisposition to side with the decisions of their subordinates and thus may violate principles of procedural justice.

This "unavailability" of political system review because of efficiency, lack of neutrality, and other reasons is an important source of injustice in public administration. The political system has at least in part passed up the opportunity for correcting bad decisions and validating good ones. Under these circumstances, the injustice can be mitigated by ensuring fair and independent review within the agency. Independent internal review is probably more common for formal adjudicative decisions, because their greater appealability to the courts and the presence of legal counsel and written procedures tend to make agencies more careful. More difficulty exists in the case of informal disputes, since legal representation and written procedures are normally lacking. Unions can help to fill the gap in the area of employee claims of injustice and therefore have an important role to play in this equation.

Internal administrative appeal systems have received great attention from both the legal profession and public employee unions. Civil service appeals procedures have been in place for many years, but the courts have been active more recently in injecting constitutional protections and fair hearing requirements (Rosenbloom, 1983b). In addition, collective bargaining has brought into many government workplaces internal grievance procedures with third-party arbitration as a final and binding step. These procedures have competed with civil service procedures, and each government jurisdiction has had to reconcile the two systems, either by making one superior to the other or by allowing the employee to elect which system to use. Not surprisingly, both systems have become increasingly judicialized. The courts have reached out through their power of judicial review to ensure uniformity and conformity to an evolving standard of constitutional due process.

Background Fairness. As appeal rights expand and deepen, new issues of Type IV injustice arise in the form of ensuring "background fairness" (Barry, 1965). These have to do with the individual's ability to enter into systems of formal justice and take full advantage of them. Does the employee or citizen have sufficient financial reserves to hire competent counsel? Does the employee wish to endure an ordeal of protracted anguish, rejection by others in the workplace, and possible retaliation by organizational managers as the price of asserting procedural rights? These are only a couple of the questions that arise. There are many well-known cases of whistleblowers who have endured hardships in order to press their claims. In many more cases, the whistle was not blown by someone who all too accurately foresaw the agonizing road ahead. What was the total cost to the public of not deciding the many questions that ought to have been raised and considered but were not?

The Civil Service Reform Act of 1978 gave to the Office of the Special Counsel within the Merit Systems Protection Board the obligation to investigate allegations by federal employees of waste, abuse, fraud, and mismanagement by public managers. The congressional investigation of the treatment of these claims reveals a human tragedy of great proportions. Not only were many of the complaints not properly investigated, but the identity of the complainant, supposedly protected under the act, was repeatedly compromised, with the result that complainants were often subjected to harsh retaliation. This sort of background unfairness makes a mockery of the formal channels of review and dissent.

Organizational Core Value Conflicts. Many injustices issues revolve around conflict among the multiple values that exist for organizing and evaluating work in the public-sector workplace. Several core values compete for dominance within public administration: political responsiveness, merit or competence, representativeness, and employee political power. Political responsiveness emphasizes the bureaucracy's role in responding to the political direction of the chief executive and the legislature, who represent the electorate. Holders of merit values believe that ability to do the job should be the primary criterion for selection, reward, and termination in the public service and that political considerations should not be allowed to enter. Representativeness focuses attention upon the need of the public service to directly reflect the general composition of the society as well as to promote the participation of a wide array of social groups in administrative decision making. The value of employee political power is sought through unionization and collective bargaining and emphasizes bilateral control of personnel policy and decision making by both agency officials and employee representatives.

These basic system values compete in ways that carry real consequences for real people. Injustice occurs, or is perceived as occurring, when persons who believe in one set of values are disadvantaged by the application of another value or combination of values. According to which core value is employed, vastly different allocations of benefits and burdens for government employees (managers, technocrats, professionals, skilled and unskilled workers alike) will flow. Who is hired and promoted and rewarded, who is disciplined and how, who is trained and why, and who is separated and when are questions of justice that constantly arise in the public workplace.

For example, merit is reflected in the civil service and position classification system laws that lays primary stress upon education and experience as job qualifications. The system does not take into account other factors, such as gender, race, age, party affiliation, and physical disability. If the value of merit is to be honored, people who believe that justice in the workplace is best served by being responsive to previously excluded racial, gender, and political groups are not as likely to come out as winners in the distribution of workplace benefits.

Proponents of political responsiveness, merit, employee political power, and representativeness have contrasting views on the issues of how agency employees should be hired, how compensation systems of public organizations should be managed, the criteria to be adopted for spending new personnel dollars, and the methods to be used in evaluating and promoting employees, among others. Inevitably, some values will prevail over others; winners and losers will emerge. In a system strongly driven by merit values, an employee who is loyal to the organization but loses out on a merit pay increase because her performance is merely adequate may feel unjustly treated. In a system favoring representativeness values, a white male employee who scores highest on a promotion examination feels deprived when he is not selected.

Summary of Understanding and
Responding to Injustice

The categorization of the types of injustice presented in this section suffers from the same handicaps as do categorization schemes in general. It attempts to force a great number of variables into a set of discrete compartments, when in reality the variables shade subtly one into the other and the categories may exclude other relevant variables.

Nonetheless, the matrix used in this chapter is useful for seeing complex phenomena more clearly and in aiding analysis and choice. Most important, a scheme for looking at administrative injustice may assist in efforts to construct administrative justice systems. The matrix helps both to locate responsibility for governmentally created injustice and to identify the nature of the injustice, and thus it points the way to corrective action.

Efforts to correct administrative injustice must go on at three levels: social, organizational, and individual. Despite the need to attack all three, public administrators are limited in the actions they can take. Given their subordinate constitutional role, they are handicapped in their ability to correct injustice arising at the level of making choices about basic social values, including the lawmaking process that goes on primarily in the three political branches of government.

The fact that the nature of injustice is political and psychological and not simply the result of a breakdown of a justice system carries important meaning for public organizations. Agencies must do more than simply implement the law and construct fair procedures to handle the myriad claims that concern citizens, external groups, and public employees. They cannot afford to stand by and be passive observers of injustice. Where they detect injustice external to the agency but caused by government, they must take advantage of their policymaking roles to seek correction. Public officials should know that much injustice is inherent in public policy, and while they may not always be in a position to vary the rules to avoid the injustice, they can pressure for change.

And where the source of injustice is beyond government, built into the fabric of society, they must not add to the injustice by being indifferent to it. Many Americans share the conviction that the bureaucracy is at best indifferent and at worst hostile to the interests of ordinary citizens. At the same time, citizens expect fair treatment from public officials and feel they have been betrayed when expectations are not met. Although it may be argued that a free society demands a citizenry that is watchful of its government agents, the absence of at least a balancing modicum of trust in the institutions of representative government is unhealthy.

How can the trust of citizens be instilled in our public administration? The assurance that one will be listened to and treated fairly is a good start. As Shklar tells us (1990, p. 90), there is no clear answer to the question of whether a citizen's complaint is authoritatively legitimate or merely subjectively so in the eyes of the citizen-complainant. It is impossible for a public official to make a plausible guess as to whether the victim has real grounds for complaint without fairly hearing her claim. If a democracy means anything at all, it means the giving of voice to its citizens and the crediting of their sense of injustice.

8

TOWARD A JUST
PUBLIC
ADMINISTRATION

In this concluding chapter we return to the themes that have concerned us throughout the book and attempt to weave them together and comment further upon them.

Injustice is ever present in the affairs of humankind and, by deduction, in government. It flows in a constant stream from sources that are, in part, linked to human motivation and self-interest and, in part, to social change, economic scarcity, and system complexity. In any society, hunger for the correction of injustice is a powerful current, but in a democratic society the surfacing of and meaningful attention to injustice claims is crucial. Facilitating the making of demands by individuals and interest groups who seek the recognition of their claims is inherent in the very nature of democracy. A process for considering claims of injustice is institutionalized in our government. The issue for us is how well injustice claims are facilitated and considered in public administration.

In the United States of the 1940s and beyond, demands that public organizations act justly toward groups and persons within the society have been channeled increasingly by our lawmakers in the direction of the courts and the legal profession, into a complex and expensive system of formal agency adjudication, grievance and antidiscrimination systems, and judicial review. But the great bulk of these demands—90 percent of them, by some informed estimates— do not gain entrance into this system. Unsystematized and often left untreated, they sow discontent and frustration and eat away at the legitimacy of public institutions. Even the claims that do receive systematic treatment in the administrative law system and are eventually "resolved" are treated in such a way that their essential political components are largely ignored.

In the preceding chapters, we presented an approach to administrative practice in public organizations that is based on the concept of administrative justice. We view the primary responsibility of public administration as comprising two essential tasks: implementing lawful public policy to achieve purposes intended by the lawmakers and dealing fairly with the claims of individuals and groups in the process. We defined "dealing fairly" mostly in terms of agency decisions but also included behaviors and even attitudes found in the bureaucracy.

The elements of administrative justice that give operational meaning to the mandate to implement lawful policy by fair means consist of a set of criteria that assesses both the outcomes and procedures of all administrative decisions, not just those specially styled as adjudication or rulemaking. We argued that we consider administrative actions to be just when the outcomes are rationally related to lawful public policy objectives; when they are accurate or correct; when they follow the formal principle of justice; when they balance rule and discretion; when they serve targeted client needs; and when they balance fairness to individuals with social or aggregate justice. We consider administrative procedures to be fair when they provide equality of access, openness and comprehensibility, impartiality, efficiency, participation and humaneness, and a meaningful right to appeal.

This conceptualization of the responsibility of public administration forms the nucleus of the administrative justice perspective that we developed throughout the book. It reflects our commitment to the principles of constitutionalism, the rule of law, democratic morality, and the rights of individuals. It also reflects our belief in the legitimate role of public administration as a "justice partner" in our constitutional system. By partnership, we convey our belief in the importance of administrative discretion and processes, the capacity of public administrators for acting justly, and the essential worthiness of our public organizations.

Because justice is a fundamental and widely shared value that can be understood and practically applied, we argued that it has considerable merit as a normative premise for administrative decision making in public organizations. We also believe that justice is an integrative concept that can incorporate the values of the public interest, social equity, and efficiency. We believe that it can reconcile a number of different efforts to find a meaningful alternative to the technical rationality paradigm, including those based on concepts of social equity, ethics and virtue, and administrative agency.

We base our approach on the recognition of the need to balance competing values, not just between justice and efficiency but also among the different elements of justice. The balance cannot be prescribed by theory or by specific guidelines for managers; rather, it must be discovered or formulated by administrators in the context of the specific roles that they play in their work settings. This requires administrators to be able to recognize justice issues in the workplace and make decisions responsive to the demands of the specific situation. Public administrators have well-developed managerial and technical skills that are reinforced by their organizations' demands for efficiency and economy. Similarly, they need to sharpen their skills in identifying and managing justice issues and to receive organizational reinforcement for their efforts to act responsibly.

Institutional support for securing administrative justice is not now commonplace. Any attempt at articulating a normative premise for administrative decision making is an ambitious undertaking that is likely to be unwelcome in some quarters and met with skepticism. Many doubtless will feel uncomfortable with our call for public administrators to become change agents for justice within their organizations, given the inhospitableness in many organizations toward anything that threatens the status quo even slightly. We recognize that acting as a change agent is risky behavior in many organizations and will demand prudence and reasoned argument. We do not intend our challenge to administrators to be easy, but, at the same time, we do not advocate professional suicide or quixotic tilting at windmills.

Reasons for Optimism

Several reasons exist to make us optimistic that we are moving in the right direction. None of these reasons is on its own sufficient to argue that administrative justice must be embraced, but taken together they comprise a brief with compelling force. These reasons may be labeled the crisis of legitimacy, the ethics movement, intellectual supports, and the demonstrated capacity and expertise of public administrators for the task of implementation.

The Crisis of Legitimacy. Early in Chapter One we spoke of the "crisis of legitimacy" in American public administration and suggested that the commitment to justice would help to address that crisis. We also argued that public administration has abandoned its fundamental responsibility for justice and must act to reclaim justice from the courts and the legal profession.

The problem of legitimacy of the bureaucracy is manifested in many different ways. One critical concern is the continued erosion of the image of the public service. In addition to impeding government's ability to act effectively, it hinders efforts to recruit "the best and the brightest" for the public service. Fortunately there are some signs that the pendulum may be starting to swing and the public service is making a comeback. After years of being the object of "bureaucrat bashing," the public service is now once again beginning to attract the interest of young professionals who want to make a contribution to society.

Many also discern a lack of legitimacy in the great discretionary latitude that public administration has enjoyed since the 1930s, symbolized by the all-too-familiar view that the bureaucracy has become a fourth branch of government, one that is out of control. Administrative justice, with its twin emphases upon constitutionalism and fair procedure, can be useful for agencies in developing rules to bound their discretion in ways that will bolster their claims to legitimacy. We agree with Kenneth Culp Davis that public administration must play a strong proactive role in bounding its own discretion. Using administrative justice principles as a guide to exercising administrative discretion can not only respond to the courts' and the public's concern about unbridled bureaucratic action, but it can help to return control for administrative justice to public administration.

The Ethics Movement. The current concern for administrative ethics is largely oriented toward curbing unethical and illegal conduct by civil servants. This feature makes it an essential part in the development of the administrative justice model, for ethical conduct is crucial in the development of the just administrator. By themselves, however, ethics-based approaches to administrative decision making do not establish tangible guidelines that will be of practical utility to managers who must make the consistent, efficient, accurate, and equal-handed decisions that justice requires.

Despite the fact that almost every issue in public administration is charged with an ethical dilemma, the executive administrator rarely has the time or the patience for constructing balanced ethical judgments (Bailey, 1962, p. 4). The hectic pace required by the role and the volume of decisions does not permit the use of vague ethics formulations. These observations support a familiar, easy-to-use normative standard for decision making. Administrative justice, as we have defined and described it, shorn of the ambiguity that attends choosing distributive standards of social justice, is a relatively easy standard to apply. It is also one that, if followed consistently, is certain to add legitimacy to administrative decisions and actions. It springs from shared attitudes and beliefs to which we can appeal in criticizing or defending public actions and policies from a moral perspective (Rawls, 1971, pp. 48–51).

If administrative ethics, as Denhardt told us (1988, p. 26), "is a process of independently critiquing decision standards, based on core values which can be discovered," then two comments are appropriate. First, administrative justice may be looked upon as a discovered set of core values that will serve as a normative framework that will "work" for most administrators. Second, if normative decision standards must be independently arrived at by each administrator, the inevitable result would be a violation of the formal principle of justice. That is, administrators would not handle equal cases alike because they would be using independent criteria. Therefore, ethics as an independent critique by morally responsible administrators is inconsistent with our approach to administrative justice: a *common set of principles binding upon all administrators.*

Nonetheless, the values and decision criteria of administrative justice do constitute an ethical approach that any administrator can adopt as a normative framework. In this sense, it competes with other normative frameworks that would be pursued by "ethical" public administrators.

Intellectual Supports. A flood of scholarly activity in various disciplines and professional fields has vastly increased interest and intellectual support for reforming and refocusing interest in administrative justice. The growth in the volume and quality of research on procedural and distributive justice by scholars in the social sciences is truly remarkable. The overwhelming impression gained from viewing this mounting intellectual output is one of increasing attention and concern to the quality of justice practiced in our organizational society.

Public administration lags far behind law, social psychology, and business administration in theoretical and empirical work on the subject of justice. Administrative justice problems are not bounded by discipline. Yet public administration has been very insular, with the result that little of the work done by other social science scholars has found its way into our literature, and vice versa. The problem goes even further, as there is little cross-fertilization of research even within academic public administration. Our profession's neglect is most apparent in the lack of scholarly interest in the empirical study of administrative justice issues.

A good part of the problem is that public administration views administrative justice, and justice generally, too narrowly. Justice is not synonymous with law or with ethics; it includes behavior, philosophy, and conflict theory and methodology. Because of the narrow view that has dominated thinking about justice issues within public administration, justice has been relegated to a lesser position as an area for scholarly inquiry. The response of academic public administration has been minimal, focusing largely on the need for education in ethics. Phillip Cooper and others speak of a resurgence of interest in law in public administration, but this has been rather limited. Moreover, we are fearful that a growth in the study of administrative law actually may be a negative: An emphasis on administrative law would reinforce the tunnel vision that we believe has been detrimental to academic public administration. It would also increase or at least continue the self-defeating subordination of administrative practice to the legal profession.

Many public administration scholars are struggling with the same issues that we have identified as central for administrative justice, albeit using different language and having different perspectives on public organizations. The thoughts and writing of Terry Cooper on virtue, of Ralph Chandler on trusteeship, of Henry Kass and Gary Wamsley on agency, and of George Frederickson on social equity are approaches that are compatible with our administrative justice perspective.

Public Administration's Capacity for Implementation. If public administration makes a commitment to justice, it has considerable expertise and resources that it can bring to the task, including knowledge of the technologies for accomplishing organizational goals as well as the requirements for responding to justice problems in specific contexts. In other words, *if* public administration focuses on instilling justice as a basic goal within our public agencies, it will succeed.

Our assessment of bureaucracy mirrors the ambivalence that Weber felt. Giving some credit to what has become for many in our field the devil incarnate doubtless reflects the deep-rootedness of technical rationality in our own thinking. But it is also a highly pragmatic recognition of the necessity and value of the bureaucratic form of government in contemporary society. More to the point, bureaucracy makes an essential contribution to fulfilling justice goals. For example, much of value for justice continues in the bureaucratic form's emphasis on equal treatment, consistency, efficiency, and accountability. Yet we remain mindful of the inherent shortcomings and dangers of bureaucracy, particularly of its tendency to dehumanize and to stress organizational rules and routines over political purpose.

Excessive judicialization and acceptance of a legalistic view of justice are harmful for public administration. Perhaps the most harmful consequence is that they shackle public administrators, freezing them out of decision situations and making it impossible for them to bring their full capabilities to bear in solving justice problems in their organizations. Justice is too important to leave to the lawyers.

Reclaiming Justice

A major role for lawyers and legal values is most viable in the formal adjudicative process, but it is less useful in rulemaking and in the informal decision and dispute settlement processes. In formal adjudication, the judiciary has a proper constitutional role to play in making sure that the agencies stay within the bounds of legislative intent and appropriately apply statutory and judicial guidelines for administrative procedure. But the courts have little experience and no practical basis for reviewing informal agency decision making.

Were they to attempt to do so, they would tie the hands of the agencies and distract them from their basic constitutional role of implementing law and public policy. This is likewise true in administrative rulemaking, which ought to proceed from political considerations and incorporate the wisdom and knowledge of public administrators as to how to achieve results through implementation.

Although the courts are overly intrusive and cannot recognize the variety of circumstances and goal criteria that affect administration, this does not mean that they have nothing to contribute. The very concept of due process, and the essential elements of fairness that it contains, should be the touchstone to be used by public administrators in dealing with citizens and public employees in its everyday affairs. Obviously, the idea of partnership can work only if public administration internalizes these guidelines for treating people fairly in the context of everyday administrative decisions. However, when applied, due process should not be limited to legally formalistic notions. The rules of notice, opportunity to be heard, neutral decision making, and appeal must be thought about in the broader context of the right to know, access to decision makers, decision makers who must balance individual cases with the achievement of policy goals, and the ability to review initial decisions and correct errors, respectively.

Even in the formal adjudicative process, legal norms and courtlike processes should not be allowed without considering their application to the administrative setting. Administrators, charged with the responsibility for seeing clearly what is required in order to achieve public policy goals, have an obligation to guard the lawmakers' intent against unthinking incursions in the name of legal formalism. The administrators' role in formal process ought to be the same as it is in informal process: to protect the lawmakers' intent and seek procedural fairness. The only difference is that in formal process there are more procedural rules to observe, and legal expertise is often essential for their correct application.

In the final analysis, partnership means an important role for both the legal profession and public administration in the business of securing administrative justice.

The Future of Just Public Administration

The role of public administration in the United States is more than the efficient implementation of public policies. Obedience to efficiency and economy, those twin instrumental values of government, would exclude from the deliberations of our administrative agencies those matters that carry the most important value claims of our citizens. For public administration to move beyond the efficiency-economy paradigm, as Dwight Waldo (1961) tells us, it will have to embrace new values that allow it to grapple with issues in human behavior and personal ethics, power and constitutional status, professional conflicts and professional ethics, and political theory and philosophy. Any new public administration paradigm that begins to address these multiple dimensions must include justice as a critical element.

Realistically, we do not foresee justice soon becoming the cornerstone of a new paradigm for American public administration. Our objectives are more modest. First, we believe the administrative justice perspective we present here can help to improve administrative practice, especially in informal agency adjudicatory decision settings. Second, we believe that it can help to balance current thinking about justice issues in public administration, thinking that is too narrowly oriented toward administrative law and its emphasis on legal norms and procedures. Expanding the traditional concept of administrative law to embrace the larger concept of administrative justice can help administrators and scholars to develop better ways to understand and solve justice problems in public organizations.

More broadly, American public administration can benefit by moving toward a more integrative theory, one that holds justice as a core value for administrative theory and practice. It is essential that the effort begin now, for the complex challenges facing American public administration in the last decade of the twentieth century and beyond will require that we address justice issues far more systematically and in much greater depth than we have thus far attempted.

REFERENCES

Adams, J. S. "Toward an Understanding of Inequity." *Journal of Abnormal and Social Psychology,* 1963, *67* (5), 422–436.

Adams, J. S. "Inequity in Social Exchange." In L. Berkowitz (ed.), *Advances in Experimental Social Psychology.* Vol. 2. New York: Academic Press, 1965.

Ad Hoc Panel on Dispute Resolution and Public Policy. *Report: Paths to Justice: Major Public Policy Issues of Dispute Resolution.* Washington, D.C.: National Institute for Dispute Resolution, Oct. 1983.

Amy, D. J. "Can Policy Analysis Be Ethical?" In F. Fischer and J. Forester (eds.), *Confronting Values in Policy Analysis: The Politics of Criteria.* Newbury Park, Calif.: Sage, 1987a.

Amy, D. J. *The Politics of Environmental Mediation.* New York: Columbia University Press, 1987b.

Appleby, P. H. *Morality and Administration in Democratic Government.* Greenwich, Conn.: Greenwood Press, 1969.

Argyris, C. *Intervention Theory and Method: A Behavioral View.* Reading, Mass.: Addison-Wesley, 1970.

Bailey, S. K. "The Public Interest: Some Operational Dilemmas." In C. J. Friedrich (ed.), *Nomos V: The Public Interest.* New York: Atherton Press, 1962.

Bailey, S. K. "The Relationship Between Ethics and Public Service." In R. C. Martin (ed.), *Public Administration and*

Democracy: Essays in Honor of Paul Appleby. Syracuse, N.Y.: Syracuse University Press, 1965.

Ball, H. *Justice Downwind: America's Atomic Testing Program in the 1950s.* New York: Oxford University Press, 1986.

Bardach, E., and Kagan, R. A. *Going by the Book: The Problem of Regulatory Unreasonableness.* Philadelphia: Temple University Press, 1982.

Barnard, C. I. *The Functions of the Executive.* Cambridge, Mass.: Harvard University Press, 1938.

Barry, B. *Political Argument.* London: Routledge and Kegan Paul, 1965.

Black, S. "The Police Department's Secret Pregnancy Test." *Washington Post,* Nov. 22, 1987, p. C8.

Bloom, A., Jr. (trans.) *Plato. The Republic.* New York: Basic Books, 1968.

Brisbin, R. A., Jr. "The Conservatism of Antonin Scalia." *Political Science Quarterly,* Spring 1990, *105,* 1–29.

Bryner, G. C. *Bureaucratic Discretion: Law and Policy in Federal Regulatory Agencies.* Elmsford, N.Y.: Pergamon Press, 1987.

Burke, J. P. *Bureaucratic Responsibility.* Baltimore, Md.: Johns Hopkins University Press, 1986.

Burnham, D. *A Law unto Itself: Power, Politics, and the IRS.* New York: Random House, 1989.

Carroll, J. D. "The New Judicial Federalism and the Alienation of Public Policy and Administration." *The American Review of Public Administration,* Spring 1982, *16,* 89–105.

CBS News. Radio report. Dec. 14, 1987.

Chandler, R. C. "Epilogue." In R. C. Chandler (ed.), *A Centennial History of the American Administrative State.* New York: Macmillan, 1987.

Chayes, A. "The Role of the Judge in Public Law Litigation." *Harvard Law Review,* 1976, *89* (7), 1281–1316.

Chitwood, S. R. "Achieving Due Process of Law: An Administrative Alternative to the Empty Promise of Formal Hearings." Southern Review of Public Administration, 1982, *6* (1), 43–64.

Clark, P. F., Gallagher, D. G., and Pavlak, T. J. "Member Commitment in an American Union." *Industrial Relations,* 1990, *21* (1), 147–157.

Cleveland, H. *The Future Executive: A Guide for Tomorrow's Managers.* New York: Harper & Row, 1972.

Cofer, D. P. "Bureaucratic Efficiency vs. Bureaucratic Justice: Administrative Law Judges in the Social Security Administration." *Judicature,* 1981, *71,* 29–35.

Cohen, R. L. (ed.). *Justice: Views from the Social Sciences.* New York: Plenum Press, 1986.

"Contempt Citations Sought Against Two U.S. Aides." *New York Times,* Apr. 8, 1988, p. 20.

Cooper, P. J. *Public Law and Public Administration.* Palo Alto, Calif.: Mayfield, 1983.

Cooper, P. J. *Public Law and Public Administration.* (2nd ed.) Englewood Cliffs, N.J.: Prentice-Hall, 1988.

Cooper, T. L. *The Responsible Administrator: An Approach to Ethics for the Administrative Role.* Port Washington, N.Y.: Kennikat Press, 1982.

Cooper, T. L. "Hierarchy, Virtue, and the Practice of Public Administration: A Perspective for Normative Ethics." *Public Administration Review,* July–Aug. 1987, *47,* 320–328.

Crosby, F. "Model of Egoistical Relative Deprivation." *Psychological Review,* 1976, *83,* 85–113.

Crosby, F., and Gonzalez-Intal, A. M. "Relative Deprivation and Equity Theories." In R. Folger (ed.), *The Sense of Injustice.* New York: Plenum Press, 1984.

Davis, J. W., Jr. *An Introduction to Public Administration: Politics, Policy, and Bureaucracy.* New York: Free Press, 1974.

Davis, K. C. *Administrative Law Treatise.* St. Paul, Minn.: West, 1958 (supplement 1970).

Davis, K. C. *Discretionary Justice: A Preliminary Inquiry.* Baton Rouge: Louisiana State University Press, 1969.

Davis, K. C. *Administrative Law and Government.* (2nd ed.) St. Paul, Minn.: West, 1975.

Deal, T. E., and Kennedy, A. A. *Corporate Cultures: The Rites and Rituals of Corporate Life.* Reading, Mass.: Addison-Wesley, 1984.

Denhardt, K. G. *The Ethics of Public Service: Resolving Moral Dilemmas in Public Organizations.* New York: Greenwood, 1988.

Denhardt, R. B. *Theories of Public Organization.* Monterey, Calif.: Brooks/Cole, 1984.

Deutsch, M. *The Resolution of Conflict: Constructive and Destructive Processes.* New Haven, Conn.: Yale University Press, 1973.

Deutsch, M. "Equity, Equality, and Need: What Determines Which Value Will Be Used as the Basis of Distributive Justice?" *Journal of Social Issues,* 1975, *31* (3), 137–149.

Deutsch, M. *Distributive Justice: A Social-Psychological Perspective.* New Haven, Conn.: Yale University Press, 1985.

Dickinson, J. *Administrative Justice and the Supremacy of Law in the United States.* New York: Russell & Russell, 1959. (Originally published 1927.)

Dimock, M. E. *Law and Dynamic Administration.* New York: Praeger, 1980.

Easterbrook, G. "Radio Free Watkins and the Crisis at Energy." *Washington Post Magazine,* Feb. 18, 1990, pp. 16–21, 33–40.

Evans, S. "Failed by Virginia Mental Health System." *Washington Post,* Nov. 23, 1987, p. A1.

Fiorino, D. J. "Regulatory Negotiation as a Policy Process." *Public Administration Review,* 1988, *48,* 764–772.

Frankena, W. K. "Some Beliefs About Justice." In J. Feinberg and H. Gross (eds.), *Justice: Selected Readings.* Encino, Calif.: Dickenson, 1975.

Frederickson, H. G. "Creating Tomorrow's Public Administration." *Public Management,* 1971, *53* (11), 2–4.

Frederickson, H. G. (ed.). "A Symposium: Social Equity and Public Administration." *Public Administration Review,* 1974, *34,* 1–51.

Frederickson, H. G. "Public Administration and Social Equity." *Public Administration Review,* Mar./Apr. 1990, *50,* 228–237.

Frederickson, H. G., and Hart, D. K. "The Public Service and the Patriotism of Benevolence." *Public Administration Review,* Sept./Oct. 1985, *45,* 547–553.

Freedman, J. O. *Crisis and Legitimacy: The Administrative Process and American Government.* Cambridge, England: Cambridge University Press, 1978.

Friedrich, C. J. "Justice: The Just Political Act." In C. J. Friedrich and J. W. Chapman (eds.), *Nomos VI: Justice.* New York: Atherton Press, 1963.

Friendly, H. J. "Some Kind of Hearing." *University of Pennsylvania Law Review,* 1975, *123,* 1267–1317.

Garland, M. B. "Deregulation and Judicial Review." *Harvard Law Review,* 1985, *98* (3), 507–591.

Gilmour, R. S. "Agency Administration by Judiciary." *Southern Review of Public Administration,* 1982, *6* (1), 26–42.

Goldberg v. Kelly, 397 U.S. 254 (1970).

Goodin, R. E. "Vulnerabilities and Responsibilities: An Ethical Defense of the Welfare State." *American Political Science Review,* Sept. 1985, *79,* 775–787.

Goodsell, C. T. *The Case for Bureaucracy: A Public Administration Polemic.* Chatham, N.J.: Chatham House, 1983.

Goss v. Lopez, 419 U.S. 565 (1975).

Graham, C. B., Jr. "The Changing Role of the Administrative Law Judge." *Public Administration Quarterly,* 1985, *9,* 260–273.

Greenberg, J. "On the Apocryphal Nature of Inequity Distress." In R. Folger (ed.), *The Sense of Injustice.* New York: Plenum Press, 1984.

Griggs v. Duke Power Company. 401 U.S. 424 (1971).

Gulick, L. "Science, Values, and Public Administration." In L. Gulick and L. Urwick (eds.), *Papers on the Science of Administration.* New York: Augustus M. Kelly, 1937.

Harmon, M. M. *Action Theory for Public Administration.* New York: Longman, 1981.

Harmon, M. M., and Mayer, R. T. *Organization Theory for Public Administration.* Boston: Little, Brown, 1986.

Harter, P. J. "Dispute Resolution and Administrative Law: The History, Needs, and Future of a Complex Relationship." *Villanova Law Review,* 1983–1984, *29* (6), 1393–1419.

Henry, N. *Public Administration and Public Affairs.* Englewood Cliffs, N.J.: Prentice-Hall, 1975.

Herring, E. P. *Public Administration and the Public Interest.* New York: McGraw-Hill, 1936.

Horowitz, D. L. *The Courts and Social Policy.* Washington, D.C.: Brookings Institution, 1977a.

Horowitz, D. L. "Courts as Guardians of the Public Interest." *Public Administration Review,* 1977b, *37,* 148–154.

Horowitz, D. L. "Decreeing Organizational Change: Judicial Supervision of Public Institutions." *Duke Law Journal,* 1983, *1983* (6), 1265–1307.

Jaffe, L. *Judicial Control of Administrative Action.* Boston: Little, Brown, 1965.

Janis, I. L. *Groupthink: Psychological Studies of Policy Decisions and Fiascoes.* (2nd ed.) Boston: Houghton Mifflin, 1982.

Kanter, R. M. "Work in New America." *Daedalus,* 1978, *107* (1), 47–78.

Kass, H. D. "Exploring Agency as a Basis for Ethical Theory in American Public Administration." *International Journal of Public Administration,* 1989, *12* (6), 949–969.

Kaufman, H. "Emerging Doctrines in the Doctrines of Public Administration." In A. A. Altshuler (ed.), *The Politics of the Federal Bureaucracy.* New York: Dodd, Mead, 1975.

Kaufman, H. *Red Tape, Its Origins, Uses, and Abuses.* Washington, D.C.: Brookings Institution, 1977.

Kelsen, H. *What Is Justice?* Berkeley: University of California Press, 1957.

Kincaid, J. "The New Judicial Federalism." *The Journal of State Government,* 1988, *61* (5), 163–169.

Kochan, T. A., and Barocci, T. A. *Human Resources Management and Industrial Relations: Text, Readings, and Cases.* Boston: Little, Brown, 1985.

Kramer, F. A. *Dynamics of Public Bureaucracy.* (2nd ed.) Cambridge, Mass.: Winthrop, 1981.

Levinson, L. H. "The Central Panel System: A Framework That Separates ALJs from Administrative Agencies." *Judicature,* 1981, *65* (5), 236–245.

Lind, E. A., and Tyler, T. R. *The Social Psychology of Procedural Justice.* New York: Plenum Press, 1988.

Lipsky, M. *Street-Level Bureaucracy: Dilemmas of the Individual in Public Services.* New York: Russell Sage Foundation, 1980.

Long, N. E. "Power and Administration." *Public Administration Review,* 1949, *9,* 257–264.

Lubbers, J. S. "Federal Agency Adjudications: Trying to See the Forest and the Trees." *Federal Bar News and Journal,* 1984, *31* (9), 383–389.

Malinski v. New York, 324 U.S. 401 (1945).

March, J. G., and Simon, H. A. *Organizations.* New York: Wiley, 1958.

Marini, F. (ed.). *Toward a New Public Administration: The Minnowbrook Perspective.* Scranton, Pa.: Chandler, 1971.

Mashaw, J. L. "The Management Side of Due Process: Some Theoretical and Litigation Notes on the Assurance of Accuracy, Fairness and Timeliness in the Adjudication of Social Welfare Claims." *Cornell Law Review,* 1974, *59,* 772–824.

Mashaw, J. L. "The Supreme Court's Due Process Calculus for Administrative Adjudication in *Mathews v. Eldridge:* Three Factors in Search of a Theory of Value." *University of Chicago Law Review,* 1976, *44* (1), 28–59.

Mashaw, J. L. "How Much of What Quality? A Comment on Conscientious Procedural Design." *Cornell Law Review,* 1980, *65,* 823–835.

Mashaw, J. L. "Administrative Due Process as Social Cost Accounting." *Hofstra Law Review,* 1981a, *9* (5), 1423–1452.

Mashaw, J. L. "Administrative Due Process: The Quest for a Dignitary Theory." *Boston University Law Review,* 1981b, *61* (4), 885–931.

Mashaw, J. L. "Conflict and Compromise Among Models of Administrative Justice." *Duke Law Journal,* 1981c, *1981* (2), 181–212.

Mashaw, J. L. *Bureaucratic Justice: Managing Social Security Disability Claims.* New Haven, Conn.: Yale University Press, 1983.

Mashaw, J. L. *Due Process in the Administrative State.* New Haven, Conn.: Yale University Press, 1985a.

Mashaw, J. L. "Prodelegation: Why Administrators Should Make Political Decisions." *Journal of Law, Economics and Organization,* 1985b, *1* (1), 81–100.

Mashaw, J. L., and others. *Social Security Hearings and Appeals.* Lexington, Mass.: Lexington Books, 1978.

Mathews v. Eldridge, 424 U.S. 319 (1976).

Merton, R. K. *Social Theory and Social Structure.* Glencoe, Ill.: Free Press, 1949.

Meyerson, M., and Banfield, E. C. *Politics, Planning and the Public Interest.* Glencoe, Ill.: Free Press, 1955.

Michels, R. *Political Parties: A Sociological Study of the Oligarchical Tendencies of Modern Democracy.* New York: Free Press, 1962.

Miewald, R. D. *Public Administration: A Critical Perspective.* New York: McGraw-Hill, 1978.

Mosher, F. *Democracy and the Public Service.* (2nd ed.) New York: Oxford University Press, 1982.

Musolf, L. *Federal Examiners and the Conflict of Law and Administration.* Baltimore, Md.: Johns Hopkins University Press, 1953.

National Commission on the Public Service, Paul A. Volcker, Chairman. *Report: Leadership for America: Rebuilding the Public Service.* Washington, D.C.: U.S. Government Printing Office, 1989.

Nonet, P. *Administrative Justice: Advocacy and Change in a Government Agency.* New York: Russell Sage Foundation, 1969.

"Northwest Pilots Were Drunk, Hill Told." *Washington Post,* Mar. 15, 1990, p. A16.

Owen v. City of Independence, 445 U.S. 622 (1980).

Perrow, C. *Complex Organizations: A Critical Essay.* (3rd ed.) New York: Random House, 1986.

Pincus, W. "Failure to Lift Clearances of North, Poindexter Hit." *Washington Post,* Nov. 9, 1987, p. A4.

Pinkele, C. F. "Discretion Fits Democracy: An Advocate's Argument." In Right Honorable Lord Denning (ed.), *The Due Process of Law.* London: Butterworths, 1980.

Pops, G. M. "An Overview of Property Assessment Review

and Appeal Systems: Goals, Variables, and Issues." *Property Tax Journal*, 1985, *4* (2), 105–128.

Pound, R. *Jurisprudence*. St. Paul, Minn.: West, 1959.

Putnam, E. "10 Million Military Medical Records Found." *Washington Post*, June 24, 1988, p. A21.

Rawls, J. *A Theory of Justice*. Cambridge, Mass.: Belknap Press, 1971.

Reagan, M. D. *Regulation: The Politics of Policy*. Boston: Little, Brown, 1987.

Redford, E. S. *Democracy in the Administrative State*. New York: Oxford University Press, 1969.

Rich, M. "Adapting the Central Panel System: A Study of Seven States." *Judicature*, 1981, *65* (5), 246–256.

Rohr, J. A. *Ethics for Bureaucrats: An Essay on Law and Values*. New York: Dekker, 1978.

Rohr, J. A. *To Run a Constitution: The Legitimacy of the Administrative State*. Lawrence: University Press of Kansas, 1986.

Roosevelt, F. D. *Message from the President of the United States Returning Without Approval the Bill (H.R. 6324) Entitled, "An Act to Provide for the More Expeditious Settlement of Disputes, and for Other Purposes."* 76th Cong., 1st sess., 1939. H. Doc. 986.

Rosenbloom, D. H. *Public Administration and Law: Bench v. Bureau in the United States*. New York: Dekker, 1983a.

Rosenbloom, D. H. "Public Administrative Theory and the Separation of Powers." *Public Administration Review*, May/June 1983b, *43*, 219–227.

Rosenbloom, D. H. "Public Administrators and the Judiciary: The 'New Partnership.' " *Public Administration Review*, 1987, *47*, 75–83.

Rourke, F. E. "Bureaucracy in the American Constitutional Order." *Political Science Quarterly*, Summer 1987, *102*, 217–232.

Runciman, W. G. *Relative Deprivation and Social Justice*. Berkeley: University of California Press, 1966.

Scalia, A. "Vermont Yankee: The APA, the D.C. Circuit, and the Supreme Court." *Supreme Court Review*, 1978, *1978*, pp. 345–409.

Schubert, G. A. *The Public Interest: A Critique of the Theory of a Political Concept.* Glencoe, Ill.: Free Press, 1960.

Schwartz, B. *Administrative Law.* Boston: Little, Brown, 1976.

Selznick, P. *Leadership in Administration: A Sociological Interpretation.* New York: Harper & Row, 1957.

Shapiro, M. "On Predicting the Future of Administrative Law." *Regulation,* 1982, *6* (3), 18–25.

Shapiro, M. *Who Guards the Guardians? Judicial Control of Administration.* Athens: University of Georgia Press, 1988.

Sheppard, B. H. "Third Party Conflict Resolution: A Procedural Framework." In B. M. Staw and L. L. Cummings (eds.), *Research in Organizational Behavior.* Vol. 6. Greenwich, Conn.: JAI Press, 1984.

Shklar, J. N. *The Faces of Injustice.* New Haven, Conn.: Yale University Press, 1990.

Sinclair, W. "Judge Rules Research Program Favors Large Farms." *Washington Post,* Oct. 19, 1987, p. A24.

Sjoberg, G., Brymer, R. A., and Farris, B. "Bureaucracy and the Lower Class." *Sociology and Social Research,* 1966, *50* (3), 325–337.

Skoler, D. L. "The Administrative Law Judiciary: Change, Challenge, and Choices." *The Annals of the American Academy of Political and Social Science,* July 1982, *462,* 34–47.

Smith, L. A. "Judicialization: The Twilight of Administrative Law." *Duke Law Journal,* 1985, *1985* (2), 427–466.

Sorauf, F. "The Conceptual Muddle." In C. J. Friedrich (ed.), *Nomos V: The Public Interest.* New York: Atherton Press, 1962.

Specter, M. "A Clash of Caution and Urgency: FDA's Drug-Approval Challenge." *Washington Post,* Oct. 26, 1987, p. A11.

Sterba, J. P. *Justice: Alternative Political Perspectives.* Belmont, Calif.: Wadsworth, 1980.

Stewart, R. B. "The Reformation of American Administrative Law." *Harvard Law Review,* 1975, *88* (8), 1667–1813.

Taylor, F. W. *Scientific Management.* New York: Harper Collins, 1947.

Thibaut, J., and Walker, L. *Procedural Justice: A Psychological Analysis*. Hillsdale, N.J.: Erlbaum, 1975.

Thibaut, J., and Walker, L. "A Theory of Procedure." *California Law Review*, 1978, *66* (3), 541–566.

Tichy, N. M. *Managing Strategic Change: Technical, Political and Cultural Dynamics*. New York: Wiley, 1983.

Tong, R. "Ethics and the Policy Analyst." In F. Fischer and J. Forester (eds.), *Confronting Values in Policy Analysis: The Politics of Criteria*. Newbury Park, Calif.: Sage, 1987.

Tribe, L. *American Constitutional Law*. Mineola, N.Y.: Foundation Press, 1978.

Tyler, T. R. "When Does Procedural Justice Matter in Organizational Settings?" In R. Lewicki, B. Sheppard, and M. Bazerman (eds.), *Research on Negotiations in Organizations*. Vol. 1. Greenwich, Conn.: JAI Press, 1986.

United States v. Morgan, 313 U.S. 409 (1941).

U.S. Congress. Attorney General's Committee on Administrative Procedure. *Final Report*. 77th Cong., 1st sess., 1941. S. Doc. 8.

U.S. Congress. *United States Statutes at Large, 1874–   , 60*, chapter 324. Washington, D.C.: U.S. Government Printing Office, 1946.

U.S. Congress. Senate. "The Landis Report." *Report on Regulatory Agencies to the President Elect*. 86th Cong., 2nd sess., 1960.

U.S. Department of Justice, Criminal Division. *A Report to the Attorney General of the United States*. Washington, D.C.: U.S. Department of Justice, Aug. 1983.

U.S. Office of Personnel Management, Office of Administrative Law Judges. *Administrative Law Judge: Program Handbook*. Washington, D.C.: U.S. Government Printing Office, 1989.

Verhovek, S. H. "Case Backlog Is Swamping Rights Agency." *New York Times*, July 17, 1989, pp. B1–B12.

Verkuil, P. R. "A Study of Informal Adjudication Procedures." *University of Chicago Law Review*, 1976, *43* (4), 739–796.

Verkuil, P. R. "The Emerging Concept of Administrative Procedure." *Columbia Law Review*, 1978, *78* (2), 258–329.

Waldo, D. *The Administrative State.* New York: Ronald Press, 1948.

Waldo, D. "Organization Theory: An Elephantine Problem." *Public Administration Review,* 1961, *21,* 210–225.

Wasserstrom, R. A. "The Case for an Equitable Decision Procedure." In J. Feinberg and H. Gross (eds.), *Justice: Selected Readings.* Encino, Calif.: Dickenson, 1975.

Weber, M. *The Theory of Social and Economic Organization.* New York: Oxford University Press, 1947.

White, L. D. *Introduction to the Study of Public Administration.* New York: Macmillan, 1926.

Wilson, J. Q. *Bureaucracy: What Government Agencies Do and Why They Do It.* New York: Basic Books, 1989.

Winerip, M. "H.U.D. Windfall: Subsidies for the Subsidized— A Special Report." *New York Times,* Dec. 31, 1989, p. 1.

Woll, P. *Administrative Law: The Informal Process.* Berkeley: University of California Press, 1963.

Wood v. Strickland, 420 U.S. 308 (1975).

Wright, J. S. "Beyond Discretionary Justice." *Yale Law Journal,* 1972, *81,* 575–597.

INDEX

191